Reading Strategies That Work

Teaching Your Students To Become Better Readers

By Laura Robb

SCHOLASTIC
PROFESSIONAL BOOKS

NEW YORK • TORONTO • LONDON • AUCKLAND • SYDNEY

For my son, Evan, and my daughter, Anina, who love to read.
For all the teachers and students I have learned with—thank you.

Cover design by Vincent Ceci and Jaime Lucero
Cover photograph by Ellen Senisi
Interior design by Solutions by Design, Inc.
Interior photographs provided by Bonnie Forstrum Jacobs
Interior illustration by James Graham Hale

Permissions
Cover illustration from *The Hallow-Wiener* by Dav Pilkey. Copyright © 1995 by Dav Pilkey.
Reprinted by permission of Scholastic, Inc.

Cover illustration from *Lily and Miss Liberty* by Carla Stevens, illustrated by Debora Kogan Kay.
Text copyright 1992 by Carla Stevens, illustrations copyright © 1992 by Deborah Kogan Kay. Reprinted by permission of
Scholastic, Inc. APPLE PAPERBACKS is a registered trademark of Scholastic, Inc.

"Our Mysteries, His Knowledge" from *Navajo: Visions and Voices across the Mesa* by Shonto Begay.
Copyright © 1995 by Shonto Begay. Reprinted by permission of Scholastic.

ISBN 0-590-25111-2

24 23 22 21 20 19 18 17 16 15   01/0

TABLE OF CONTENTS

ACKNOWLEDGEMENTS

As the idea for this book began to take shape in my mind, many people supported me.

Thanks, first, goes to my husband, Lloyd, who listened to constant talk about reading strategies and who patiently read, questioned, and reread each draft. Never once did he complain when I spent long hours writing and thinking in my office.

To Terry Cooper, my editor at Scholastic, for seeing the importance of this topic and supporting me as I wrote and revised.

I am grateful to Ann Tobias, my agent, for her expert suggestions which brought clarity to each chapter.

Thanks to all the teachers who invited me into their classrooms to work with children in grades two through six and develop a strategic reading program. To my son Evan Robb, to Liz Davies, Marti Chapman, and Peggy Wampler, all teachers in Clarke County Public Schools who worked closely with me to support children's reading. To Carol Chapman, Ellen Benjamin, Nancy Roche, and Lynne Lacy, all colleagues at Powhatan School whose belief in teaching reading through strategies sustained me through years of classroom research.

Finally, I'd like to recognize the children who shared their thinking with me and gave me an abundance of suggestions to reflect upon. The children helped me revise and refine my understanding of each strategy, and they continue to do so as we learn together and explore new directions.

INTRODUCTION

In 1990, I began working with second- and sixth-grade reluctant readers, students who could pronounce the words in a text, but disliked and avoided reading. Time and again these children described their feelings toward reading with adjectives such as *boring, pointless, dumb*. "You can't make me read," they often told me, with defiance and anger. How right they were! There was no way I could force these students to read beyond saying the words in the book.

That year, to gain insight into these students' reading lives, I interviewed the children, and tape-recorded the conversations so I could listen to them again and again. My goal was to understand why these students disliked and avoided reading and then develop teaching interventions that could change their attitudes and behavior.

In the five years since that first round of interviews, I have interviewed close to three hundred boys and girls ranging from reluctant readers to gifted. The information I collected from these conversations has enabled me to understand how this group of elementary- and middle-school students approached reading problems and why so many of them—regardless of their reading abilities—stated, "reading is just something you do for school."

What I discovered is that the children who avoid reading never connected to a book in a deep and meaningful way. Moreover, most had no idea how they could connect to the information in nonfiction or enter into a character's life. Many complained that they had difficulty recalling information from textbooks.

These children led me to rethink some popular reading beliefs. I came to realize that it isn't enough to offer children the finest literature. Putting the right book into a child's hand does not guarantee that the child will engage with it—and it rarely transforms a reluctant reader into an avid reader. To bring children and books together successfully, children have to experience the pleasures of reading. They have to hear stories, make predictions, visualize characters, talk about plot twists, imagine story settings, emotionally respond to characters, and think with new information. I developed the Strategic Reading Program to provide a framework for giving students these reading experiences.

As you read this book, you'll explore a menu of reading strategies to offer students that foster independence in reading and help bond children to books. Like you, I want every child to love real books and develop a rich and varied personal reading life. A strategic reading program not only recognizes the transforming power of literature, but it also acknowledges that you and I have to give children helpful support as we nudge them to become lifelong readers.

CHAPTER 1

The Difference Between Reading Skills and Reading Strategies

"**I** read words—don't expect me to think!" fifth-grader Josh said to me, his voice heavy with frustration, when I asked him why he never wrote about choice reading in his dialogue journal. For Josh, reading was simply decoding, and he was able to pronounce the words in very difficult texts. What Josh lacked was the ability to recollect what he had read. Recall was difficult for Josh because he did not have the reading strategies that would help him connect the text's information to what he already knew about a subject. Consequently, he would plunge into a text and quickly turn off. That's why, for Josh, reading had become "something you do for school, but not fun."

Josh had never thought about the purposes of reading, let alone the pleasure and entertainment books can offer. "I can read all the words," he said, "but I still get low grades."

Students like Josh, who, technically speaking, can read, made me pause and ask myself: What is the act of reading? Before deciding what kinds of instruction to offer students, I believe it's important for each of us to answer this question for ourselves. With a clearer notion of what reading is, we are better able to help students see the value and purposes of reading in their lives.

For me, reading is like a conversation between two people. It's a dialogue between reader and author. Good readers bring their knowledge and experiences to an author's words to help them understand and recall the text. Good readers, like good conversationalists, are able to use the information to arrive at a deeper understanding of something. They don't merely recall what they read, they *comprehend* it. They apply past knowledge and experiences to the information in a text and create new understandings, solve problems, and make connections to other texts and experiences.

So What Is Strategic Reading?

To define strategic reading, I go back to the difference between skills and strategies. The distinction between skills and strategies is one my colleagues and I have often discussed. Traditionally, "skills" has described a set of helpful tools that students practiced in order to improve reading. (They include, but are not limited to: vocabulary in context, sequencing, making inferences, coping with unfamiliar words, and many more.)

While I have chosen to teach skills in the context of authentic literature, and basal readers frequently organize the skills sequentially for students to practice in isolated drills, many of the skills themselves have not changed. What has changed, for me, is the understanding that skills and strategies are shades of the same thing—but representing different stages of development.

I believe that a skill becomes a strategy when the learner can use it independently, when she can reflect on and understand how it works and then apply it to new reading materials. When this occurs, the student has become what I consider a strategic reader.

You can help students move their use of skills to the level of strategies by:

> *Organizing guided practice around the authentic reading materials students use at school and home. Include stories, parts of novels and*

nonfiction books, newspaper and magazine articles, and textbooks.

> *Helping students reflect on the skills you introduce by inviting them to talk and write about how they are using them. Heightening students' awareness of how a skill works moves them toward applying it independently.*

> *Observing and thinking about each child's progress. Work with students to decide whether they need additional practice or are ready to try using the skill on their own.*

> *Offering students opportunities to independently apply what they've learned during guided practice to books they are reading.*

What Good Readers Can Do

The reluctant readers I interviewed essentially gave up when they hit a confusing passage, an unknown word, or a book that was too difficult for them. Obviously, they had never discovered the supportive reading strategies that we know good readers use.

As you think about which strategies to present to your students, periodically review the following list of characteristics of proficient readers. I find revisiting the list refreshes my memory as I choose specific student behaviors to observe during reading, and helps me plan my teaching goals.

STRATEGIES AND BEHAVIORS OF GOOD READERS

BEHAVIOR	READING STRATEGY
Uses imagery to understand and enjoy reading.	Visualization
Chooses a book appropriate to reading level.	Book selection
Knows the purpose of the text and can set own purposes for reading.	Skimming; Questioning; Predicting
Predicts, then reads to confirm or adjust predictions.	Making Predictions
Recalls details of what she's read.	Pausing/Summarizing; Retelling; Note-taking
Adjusts reading rate for task and text.	Monitoring Reading Rate; Skimming
Clears up confusing parts.	Rereading; Thinking-aloud; Using Context Clues
Asks questions and reads to answer these questions.	Questioning; Setting Purposes; Rereading; Skimming
Selects and uses new and interesting vocabulary from texts.	Using Context Clues; Skipping, Going on, and Rereading; Expanding Word Knowledge
Uses information to think and make connections.	Finding explicit or inferred data in text to support ideas; Note-taking
Inquires to further understand information in text.	Reflecting; Questioning; Rereading
Uses text to discover unstated meanings.	Inferring; Concluding; Noting Cause/Effect; Comparing/Contrasting
Seeks help when needed.	Self-monitoring
Accesses what she already knows about different text structures.	Using Prior Knowledge

> With a strategic approach to reading, you'll teach students to apply these strategies while reading novels, nonfiction, textbooks, magazines, charts, and any other text. You'll help them gradually move toward a point where using the strategies is "second nature."

Which Strategies Do I Teach?

It's difficult to develop hard and fast guidelines for teaching specific strategies at each grade level. So much depends upon what students know when they arrive in our classrooms, and this changes each year.

One group of teachers in grades two through six decided to create a "strategy teaching plan" prior to the second year of using the strategic reading model. During the first year, each teacher kept a log of strategies introduced and practiced and used their notes to design the plan on page 11.

Strategic Reading: How It Fits into a Comprehensive Reading Program

The Strategic Reading Program outlined in this book is one key element of a comprehensive reading program, which, among other things, includes lots and lots of time for choice reading and talking about literature. To give you an idea of how the strategic reading program fits into a reading curriculum, take a look at the Key Elements list that follows. Of course, you will not cover everything each day, but during the school year, stu-

dents will have opportunities to experience the diverse elements. For example, within a one and one-half hour daily block of time, I schedule 45 minutes of both guided reading and literature discussion groups twice each week; children have choice reading four times each week for 30 to 45 minutes. The following list will show you where Strategic Reading fits into a comprehensive reading program.

Some Key Elements Of A Comprehensive Reading Program

DIVERSE READING EXPERIENCES

- *Free Choice Reading*
- *Daily Read Alouds*
- *Guided Reading*
- *Reading to Research*

A RANGE OF MATERIALS

- *Children's Literature*
- *Core Reading Materials*
- *Magazines, charts, schedules, brochures, pamphlets, students' writing*

(continued on page 11)

THE STRATEGIC READING PROGRAM

- **Two Guided Practice Sessions Each Week**
- **Reading Strategy Minilessons**
- **Vocabulary and Word Study**
- **Students' Reading Strategy Logs**
- **Debriefings and Conferences**

GRADE 2	GRADE 3	GRADE 4
Predict	Predict	Predict
Retell	Retell	Question
Question	Question	Reread
Reread	Reread	Read-Pause-Retell
Vocabulary: Guessing	Vocab. Webs	All Vocab. Strategies
Browse	Vocab. Discussion	Skim
K-W-H-L	Charts	Brainstorm
Vocab. Connections	Vocab. Connections	Visualize
Visualize	K-W-H-L	Fast Write
Brainstorm	Visualize	Bookmarks
Bookmarks	Bookmarks	Reading Rate
Skim	Read-Pause-Retell	K-W-H-L
Reading Rate	Reading Rate	Cause/Effect
Cause/Effect	Cause/Effect	Context Clues
Context Clues	Context Clues	Confusing parts
Identify confusing parts	Confusing parts	Self-correct
Self-correct	Self-correct	Venn Diagram
Book Selection	Venn Diagram	Book Selection

GRADE 5	GRADE 6
Summarize	Summarize
Fast Write	Skim
All of grade 4	Note-taking
Review all strategies when necessary	Review all strategies when necessary.

Key Elements of Comprehensive Reading Program, cont'd.

📖 *Basal Readers and Content Textbooks*

RESPONDING TO READING

📖 *Literature Discussion Groups*

📖 *Fostering Reading-Writing Connections*

Responding to Reading, cont'd.

📖 *Journal Writing*

📖 *Book Talks*

📖 *Reader's Theater*

📖 *Drama*

📖 *Art*

Continued on page 12

- 📖 *Music*
- 📖 *Dance*

WRITING

- 📖 *Learning About Writing from Reading*
- 📖 *Writing in a Range of Genres*
- 📖 *Choice Writing: Students Generate Topics*
- 📖 *Teacher-directed Writing*
- 📖 *Writing Technique*
- 📖 *Writing to Learn Content*
- 📖 *Critical Analysis*

ON-GOING ASSESSMENTS

- 📖 *Debriefings and Conferences*
- 📖 *Self-evaluations*
- 📖 *Teacher's Observations and Notes*
- 📖 *Students' Writing*
- 📖 *Students' Reading Strategy Logs*

As a strategic reading teacher, your goal is to help students apply the strategies independently before, during, and after reading, in school and at home. But there is no one correct route to reach this goal. Through reading conferences and interviews, classroom observations, and students' reading strategy logs, you'll be able to evaluate students' progress and needs, then decide which strategies to teach in depth and which to touch on lightly. In other words, you will create your own road map as you provide for differences in students' learning styles, experiences, and abilities. The following outline of a strategic reading program will help get you started.

A Model for Strategic Reading

I developed what I call the Strategic Reading Program to meet the needs of all those students who are indifferent or decidedly turned off to reading. What emerged is a teaching model that moves beyond students' observations and discussion of what I modeled. Students taught me that a demonstration wasn't enough! Teacher modeling and thinking out loud are only the first steps to understanding and integrating strategies into purposeful reading. The others are listed below.

Implementing the Strategic Reading Program

1 **Assess Prior Knowledge:** Ask students what they know about a strategy. Have them write their thoughts in their strategy log.

This will help you decide what to include in your demonstration.

2 **Select a Strategy:** Prepare a minilesson that carefully explains a strategy.

3 **Demonstrate/Discuss:** Present a minilesson to the whole class or small groups, modeling the way the strategy works. Invite students to share how the strategy works—or doesn't work—for them. Record students' ideas on chart paper.

4 **Offer Guided Practice:** Using books from a variety of genres,

provide students opportunities twice a week to work through a strategy under your guidance. Write students' responses on chart paper. Offer students enough guided practice until they can discuss the strategy and demonstrate an understanding of how it works. Using different texts, continue to practice with small groups or individuals if they need additional support, or ask a student to coach them.

5 **Invite Self-evaluation:**
Invite students to write about the strategy in their logs, explaining it and discussing how it helps.

6 **Encourage Independence:**
Provide opportunities for students to apply the strategy on their own—while reading at school and at home.

7 **Evaluate/Respond:**
Use the data that you gather from students' independent work to assess them and to guide your instruction.

What Is the Purpose of Guided Practice?

Guided practice may not be as well-known as the other strategies in the program, so I will discuss it briefly here. Because guided practice is the "glue" that holds the strategic reading program together, it's important to understand what it is and what it does for students. Guided practice allows you to isolate key reading strategies and help students gain a deeper understanding of how a strategy can support reading. While students practice and use

strategies, they can experience ways that strategies work together. These twice-a-week sessions often begin with a minilesson that shows students how a particular reading strategy helps you. For example, you might use a nonfiction book on planets to explain how you recall information to answer a factual question about Mars, and also to share how you use factual information from a text to make inferences about other planets in the solar system. Showing students the way you approach reading tasks and spotlighting how specific strategies help you, offers kids a concrete model to observe and think about.

The demonstration, or minilesson, is just one part of guided practice. Below are a variety of experiences your students can explore during guided practice.

Suggestions for Guided Practice Sessions

- *Planned and spontaneous teacher minilessons*
- *Planned student-presented minilessons*
- *Discussions of students' questions and observations*
- *Whole-group practice with strategy*
- *Small-group and partners practice*
- *Students' independent practice*
- *Debriefings (public discussions) about a strategy after teacher-led practice and students' independent practices*
- *Conferences*
- *Student reflections in their Reading Strategy Logs (Please see*

page 25 for more about managing these notebooks.)

Placing Reading Strategies in the Three-Part Reading Model

T o develop students' reading power to the fullest, you'll invite learners to apply strategies before, during, and after reading.

Strategies used before reading activate what learners already know and have experienced. Strategies employed while reading emphasize understanding and recalling information. Post-reading strategies invite students to reason and think with text information, make connections to other situations, enlarge vocabulary, gain new information, and question to learn more.

Some Closing Thoughts

As you launch a strategic reading program in your classroom, you will constantly rely on your personal reading experience to guide you. To keep you attuned to your own reading habits, here are some questions to ask yourself from time to time. I find they help

STRATEGIES TO USE BEFORE READING	STRATEGIES TO USE WHILE READING	STRATEGIES TO USE AFTER READING
[*These activate past knowledge and experiences.*]	[*These use past knowledge to recall and understand.*]	[*These expand past knowledge and help create new understandings.*]
Brainstorm	Reading Rate	Confirm, Adjust Predictions
Predict	Predict	Skim
Browse	Questions	Visualize
Skim	Reread	Question
Question	Summarize	Reread
Vocabulary Predictions	Self-Correct	Think-Aloud
Vocabulary Web	Visualize	Retell
Fast Write	Identify Confusing Parts	K-W-H-L
K-W-H-L	K-W-H-L	Note-Taking
	Monitor Vocabulary	Reflect Through: Writing, Talking, Dance and Movement, Drawing
	Monitor Understanding	
	Context Clues	Venn Diagram
	Bookmarks	Infer
	Seek Help	

me step inside students' shoes and consider feelings about reading from their points of view.

- 📖 *What do I do when I come upon an unfamiliar word?*

- 📖 *Why do I enjoy some books more than others?*

- 📖 *How do I select free-choice books?*

- 📖 *What keeps me interested in a book?*

- 📖 *Why do I abandon a book I have begun to read?*

- 📖 *Why do some students never choose to read for pleasure?*

- 📖 *What similarities and differences do I see among children who relish reading and those who dislike reading?*

In the next chapter, you'll explore your reading life in more detail, and discover ways to incorporate what you do as a reader into your teaching.

Students and Teachers Share the Same Reading Process

Know Yourself as a Reader

W hen I lead staff development sessions on the reading process, I hand out professional journal articles and ask my colleagues to read them—right then and there. As they read, I watch what they do, and take notes on an overhead transparency. Below are some behaviors I often note:

- 📖 *Skims text before reading*
- 📖 *Takes notes in margin*
- 📖 *Takes notes in journal*
- 📖 *Rereads*
- 📖 *Underlines some passages*
- 📖 *Pauses*

- 📖 *Puts a question mark in margin*
- 📖 *In journal writes "schemata?"*
- 📖 *Whispers to a colleague*
- 📖 *Finishes early—rereads selected parts*
- 📖 *Everyone completes reading at different times*
- 📖 *Holds finger on one page and rereads from another page.*

When everyone is done reading, I flash the list on a screen. Together, we marvel at how much we already know about reading strategies. And invariably, my colleagues find that they all use more than one strategy to understand and remember what they read.

Next I invite them to gather in small

groups to talk about why they used the strategies they did. The list below illustrates the power of teacher reflection:

📖 *I paused to think about what I had already read.*

📖 *Writing helped clarify ideas.*

📖 *Writing helps me remember better.*

📖 *I put a question mark to show I didn't understand.*

📖 *I skimmed before I read to get an idea about the content.*

📖 *I underlined what I thought was important to know.*

📖 *I reread what wasn't clear the first time.*

📖 *I talked to ask a question.*

📖 *I talked to show a friend a part that spoke to me.*

📖 *I looked back to check on a fuzzy part.*

If you teach reading strategies, it's crucial to understand how strategies work while *you* read. To get in touch with your reading process, cultivate the habit of reflecting on what you do as a reader, then asking yourself why you do it. By thinking deeply about the process, you'll gain valuable insights and observations to pass on to students.

Discover What Your Students Know

Once you see the benefits of thinking about yourself as reader, you'll want to encourage students to do the same. Those students who have insights into their reading process can improve when they identify what they can do well and what they need to improve. After students practice and apply a strategy, invite them to share "how they do it." Asking students to talk about how a strategy works offers learners different ways to solve the same problem.

The Reading Strategy Interview

Conducting reading interviews is one of the first things you'll do to launch your strategic reading program. These interviews help you quickly document students' knowledge of reading strategies. During the interviews, you'll ask children questions like those shown on page 19, and record their responses on the Reading Interview Form (see figure 1, page 21). You'll use the completed interviews to guide your first conferences with students and to write notes about what students already know about reading.

The nature of the notes you take will change with each class and grade level because every group of children arrives with different experiences and background knowledge. To illustrate, in 1994, I worked with fourth,- second-, and sixth-graders. After conducting and reviewing strategy interviews, I began guided practice: the fourth-grade class started with strategies that help understand unfamiliar words, the second-grade class with retelling, and the sixth-graders, all reluctant readers, with making predictions. Each year you'll face new challenges because you're starting where students are in their reading development, rather than forcing students into a prescribed plan.

Suggestions for Interview Questions

BOOK SELECTION

Why do you check out a book to read?

How do you know if you can read the book?

BEFORE READING

Now that you have a book to read, do you do anything before you start reading?

WHILE READING

If you are alone and can't pronounce a word, what do you do?

If you are alone and don't know what a word means, what do you do?

What do you do if you don't understand a paragraph or an entire page?

AFTER READING

Now that you have completed the book, what do you do?

Preparing for the Interviews

Interviews take about ten minutes per student. Try to complete two to three each day. Take the time to establish behavior guidelines for students to follow while you're conferring, and post these on a chart for all to see. Make sure students know what projects they can be working on, as well as the acceptable ways to receive assistance from peers. (Please see page 25 for more on peer-help guidelines.)

Tips To Help Students Relax During the Interview

Find a place inside the classroom or just outside the door where you can confer privately. Explain that you're collecting information to help them improve reading. Emphasize that there are no right or wrong answers to the questions.

Spend a few minutes chatting with students. Ask questions that encourage them to talk about hobbies, friends, sports, clothes, favorite foods, games, movies etc.

Explain that you will be taking notes in order to remember the conversation. Assure them that they will be able to read your notes.

Be a good listener. Whenever you feel you need more information, ask follow-up questions that encourage students to elaborate.

Record what students say without paraphrasing or editorializing.

The dialogue on page 20 is the heart of an interview with a second-grader named Hunter.

After I reread this interview, I listed all the strategies Hunter was consciously using in the Notes section of the form. I recorded that Hunter knew how to determine if he could read a book, knew what kinds of books he wanted to check out, and thought about the book after reading, sometimes drawing pictures of favorite parts. Two goals I noted were to help Hunter use predictions

MY READING INTERVIEW WITH HUNTER

Robb: Why do you choose a book to read?

Hunter: I look for scary stories--they're my favorite.

Robb: How do you know you can read the book?

Hunter: You try to read the title and one page. If you can read the whole page by yourself, the book is right for you.

Robb: Now that you have your book, do you do anything before you start to read?

Hunter: Before I open it I read the title and author. Then I start.

Robb: If you are alone and can't pronounce a word, what do you do?

Hunter: I try to sound it out.

Robb: What do you when you sound out a word?

Hunter: I sound it out.

Robb: If you are alone and don't know what a word means, what do you do?

Hunter: I skip it and see if I can get it when I read on. I ask someone or I might put the book back.

Robb: What do you do if you don't understand a paragraph or an entire page?

Hunter: I would think the book's too hard.

Robb: Do you try anything?

Hunter: I never try to figure hard parts out. I get a different book.

Robb: Now that you've completed the book, what do you do?

Hunter: Sometimes I think about it before I go to bed. I think of the pictures or parts I liked--like real scary parts. Sometimes I draw pictures.

before and during reading, and to offer some strategies for coping with a confusing portion of a text and words he couldn't pronounce.

At our first five-minute mini-conference, which took place *after* the interview, Hunter and I discussed what he was doing that supported his reading. Together we set two goals for him: to make predictions before and during reading, then confirm or adjust these; to learn strategies that deal with confusing parts of a text.

Filing and Using Interviews

Store each interview sheet in a reading conference folder. You and students can return to these to discuss progress half-way through the school year and at its end. Record students' remarks and any pertinent comments you make. Some samples follow.

Louise's Reflections

At the beginning of third grade, the two

strategies Louise spoke of were, "sounding out a word I can't say," and "before I read the book I think, what will it be about?" In the Reading Interview Form shown below, note fourth-grader Louise's ability to talk about the strategies she uses. What growth she experienced after a year of strategic teaching!

Once I've completed the interviews, I record all the strategies my students are using on a large chart and post it. My students and I discuss the list; I emphasize how much they already know about what good readers do. Here is a chart from a fourth-grade class:

— I read the front and back covers to decide if I like a book.

— Sometimes I try to guess what the book will be about before I start it.

(continued on page 22)

READING INTERVIEW FORM

NAME: Louise   **DATE:** 9/19/94   **GRADE:** 4

1. BOOK SELECTION STRATEGIES

I look for horse stories and fairy tales.

I use the 5-finger way—if I can't say or don't know 5 words on a page, then I say, "Read that later."

2. BEFORE READING STRATEGIES

I read the title and author. I think about the cover picture and look for other pictures in the book. I predict what it will be about.

3. DURING READING STRATEGIES

I see if there are small words in the word I can say. Or I read on and go back to see if I can say it.

I can figure out a word I don't understand if I read on or read what came before or look at pictures.

I read a part lots of times if I don't understand. Sometimes I get Janie to help cause she can read anything.

4. AFTER READING STRATEGIES

I like to pretend I'm a character. If it's a fairy tale, I make a play and make my brother do some parts. I reread parts I really like.

NOTES: Strengths: Uses 5-finger method; rereads to figure out confusing parts; uses context to understand new vocabulary; predicts before reading; reflects on book after reading; rereads; self-monitors.

GOALS: To confirm and adjust predictions during and after reading; to use questioning and visualization; to discuss strategies L. uses with textbooks.

Figure 1

— I reread parts I don't understand lots of times until I get it.

— If I can't say a word I look for parts I can say and try to put them together. Sometimes I ask a person in my group to help me.

— I reread parts of the book I really liked.

— I reread a hard book three or four times—until I get all of it.

— I write my own stories about the characters I loved.

— I look at the pictures a lot before and after I read.

Discover How Students See Themselves as Readers

Beyond learning about students' strategies, find out how they view themselves as readers. This will help you prepare for conferences, recommend book titles, pair students up who can help one another, and set reasonable goals for your students. Here are seven questions that can help students think and discuss their feelings about reading.

SEVEN QUESTIONS ABOUT READING

1 Why do you read?

2 What benefits do you see in reading?/ How do you think reading helps you?

3 What do you do well as a reader?

4 Do you read at home? How often? What do you read?

5 How does reading make you feel?

6 What are some of your favorite books?

7 Do you have a favorite author? Why do you enjoy this author's books?

Model How You Want Students to Respond

Before you ask students to respond to the questions, take a few days to show them how *you* would answer them. This will yield more reflective responses from students. I prefer such responses in the form of narratives as shown in the samples here; however, responses can take the form of a question and answer— question and response to each question.

Guidelines for Modeling

Day One: Using a colored marker pen, write the seven questions on three pieces of large chart paper, leaving room between questions for your notes. In front of the class, talk about how you would respond to the questions. Jot notes on the paper. As you write, think out loud so students can hear and see how you decide where to place notes on the chart.

Day Two: Read aloud your notes to the class. Add any new ideas that come to you.

Day Three: Use your notes to write your final responses on the chart paper. Use a different color marker pen so students can easily differentiate the questions and answers. Post the chart for students to use as a reference.

Invite students to ask questions about your responses. Then have them work in groups to write initial notes for each of the seven questions. Tell students that if they have no answer to a question, they should write "no response." Allow three to four periods to complete, depending on the age and development of the group. Younger students can answer each question separately with words and pictures or pictures only. Set up a short conference and take notes on their explanations.

What You Can Learn from Students' Responses

Some children will answer all questions; others will skip several. One sixth-grader I worked with did not list one thing she did well as a reader. During a follow-up chat Nikita told me, "I'm always the last to finish [a reading assignment] in class. I'm so slow, how can I have any good points?"

"Do you understand and remember what you read?" I asked.

"Sure," she replied. "But reading fast means you're good."

Responses like Nikita's open the door for conversations about reading strengths and signal the need for strategy lessons on reading rate, skimming, and previewing.

As I did with Nikita, try to find out why a student has skipped a question. As you can tell from the answers of Sally (fourth-grade) and Jeffrey (fifth-grade)—and my thoughts about them (which I write on stick-on notes)—the seven questions yield insights into the reading lives of students. (Figures

2¹–2⁴ below.) The students' responses tell you so much of what you need to know, helping you find learning situations that will play to each student's strengths while you build up their use of every strategy.

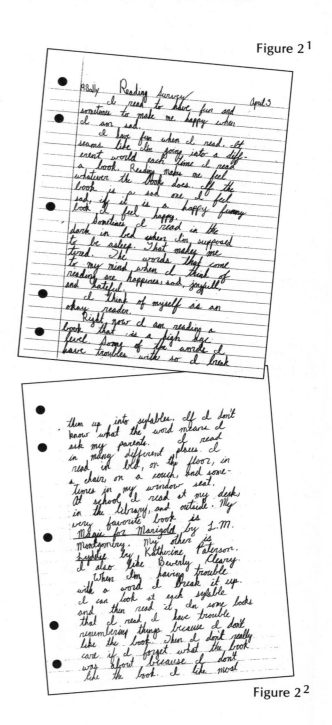

Figure 2¹

Figure 2²

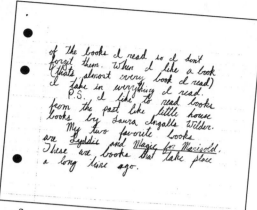

Figure 2 [3]

Sally-Grade 4. Joyful, thoughtful reader.
Reads a great deal in different places- books
important part of Sally's life. Has strategies
to pronounce unfamiliar words. Why
"hateful"? Get Sally to clarify. Has developed
tastes. Use, possibly, as a peer helper.

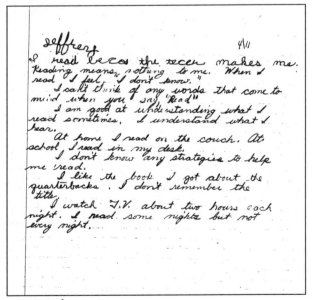

Figure 2 [4]

Jeffrey-Grade 5
Tell Jeffrey how much you appreciate his
honesty. Glad he reads at home. Do an
independent reading inventory to try to find
out why he feels "I don't know." Conference
ASAP to discuss mixed messages and try to
get more data.

Using Student Interviews in Planning

I store my notes from the reading strategy interviews and students' responses to the seven questions about reading in a planning journal. (I use an extra-thick spiral notebook with several storage pockets for separate papers. A three-ring looseleaf binder will work well, too.) Here is what I keep in my planning journal:

- *Stick-on notes based on interviews and responses to the seven questions about reading. (Sample boxes under figures 2[3] and 2[4], this page.)*

- *A list of possible strategy minilessons for whole class, small groups, or individual students.*

- *Notes and brainstorming for specific strategy minilessons that I am preparing.*

- *Students' comments and important questions on minilessons we've worked on.*

- *My reactions to minilessons that I have modeled.*

- *Notes on possible ways to support different students.*

- *Titles of books and stories suitable for practice.*

I utilize the information in my journal as well as classroom observations to create and constantly update a student-centered teaching plan. During the first two months of the school year, I find that I jot notes almost daily in my planning journal because I am interviewing students, reading their responses to the seven questions, and holding brief conferences. As the year progresses, and I begin to focus on small groups who require extra help, the task of maintaining the journal becomes easier. Since rereading my notes helps me find ways to help students, I reread the planning book often.

The Student Reading Strategy Log

This is a booklet students make by stapling about 20 pieces of lined composition paper between two pieces of colored construction paper. In the log, students keep a written record of each strategy they have studied and practiced. They also evaluate how each strategy supports their reading. You can see how helpful self-evaluations are from the following excerpts from strategy logs.

— Predicting makes me want to read more. (Jessica, Grade 3)

— I like to ask questions about the book before I read. That makes me curious to find out more. (Bobby, Grade 5)

— Rereading helps me remember fact after fact in science. (Harold, Grade 6)

— When I retell a book I ask myself if I remembered a lot. If I say 'No' then I go back and read it until I can tell the story. (Ginna, Grade 2)

When Students Write in the Logs

Students use their strategy logs during every guided practice session; for homework I sometimes ask them to write about ways they integrate a strategy or strategies into all kinds of reading. Keeping students' responses in one place allows you and them to monitor—and appreciate—how much progress they have made.

I reread the logs frequently, for they offer insights that I need to support and celebrate each child's progress. I never write in students' strategy logs; we discuss contents during brief conferences. When I return the logs to students, I like to make a positive comment about what I've noticed. When I say things like, "I noticed how you were able to give terrific evidence that supported your prediction," or "I know it's hard. sometimes, to get a mental picture of a word, and I appreciate your effort," students know that I value their thinking and hard work.

The strategy log, *along with other student work*, provides the evidence you need for documenting each child's progress. Share the log with parents and administrators so they can see the amount of learning that has taken place.

Ways to Help Kids Coach Kids

How can I possibly help every child progress when I have twenty-five students with different needs? That's a question you and I constantly wrestle with as we try to construct student-centered learning communities. Using peer helpers can greatly diminish your stress as you work with one to two groups. And it quickens the pace of learning, too.

Early in the year, students and I establish an I-Need-Help Procedure Chart (sample on page 26). The chart hangs on a wall, and students read it out loud periodically to refresh everyone's memory. (Reviewing is especially helpful prior to conferencing.)

I-NEED-HELP PROCEDURE CHART

If you need help, do the following in a soft, learning voice:

1. Think for a moment. Try to solve the problem yourself.

2. Ask your group for support.

3. If a group member can't help, ask a student you think can help you.

4. If none of the above work, ask the teacher.

Students can work together during guided practice sessions and other class times. Below are some ways you can organize pairs so that you can attend to those students who require your support. Partners can:

- *Prepare minilessons to present to classmates.*

- *Practice repeated readings.*

- *Read and exchange predictions and questions.*

- *Think aloud to understand a difficult text.*

- *Practice and monitor a strategy.*

- *Retell stories.*

- *Prepare a vocabulary web or map.*

Sometimes I select partners; at other times students choose. Vary partnerships so children learn with different classmates. The information you collect from strategy logs, interviews, guided practice, students' responses to the seven questions, and your daily observations will enable you to establish partnerships and small teams of students who can work productively and help one another.

Some Closing Thoughts

Knowing yourself as a reader can help as you invite students to reflect on themselves as readers. You can share your thoughts and experiences with them.

Give yourself several weeks to complete the reading interviews. With experience you will gain speed and the knack of short-hand notations; all you need is a word or phrase that jogs your recall of the full answer.

Take time to absorb the information from the interviews and the seven reading questions. Read and reflect on one or two each day so you won't be overwhelmed. You may find yourself focusing on the few students who express negative attitudes toward reading and seem unaware of any strategies.

Use the data to organize peer support networks. There is no better way to endorse the joy of reading than to have kids talk with one another about books and how they get the most out of what they read.

The Minilesson and Beyond

What Is a Minilesson?

Developed by Nancie Atwell and Lucy Calkins, the minilesson is a brief, focused session—usually just 10 to 15 minutes—that teaches strategies through demonstration. Thinking out loud and writing in front of students, the presenter models the way a particular strategy works.

The purpose of these information-packed monologues is to allow learners to observe firsthand how a peer or the teacher uses a strategy. A lively discussion follows each minilesson. Students exchange ideas, ask questions, and share how they use and apply the strategy.

The real strength of a minilesson is in the follow-up discussions, for that is when students swap stories about their reading struggles and strengths, and in so doing, the strategies become more meaningful to them.

Chart Paper: The Blank Canvas of a Minilesson

Whether I'm giving an impromptu minilesson or one I've planned, I write all of my minilessons on large chart paper. I prefer chart paper to writing on an overhead transparency because I can easily display the charts on the walls, and they are easy for students to reread. The charts, which represent a dynamic collaboration between the presenter and students, become a powerful resource for everyone.

The Roles of Presenter and Observer During a Minilesson

The presenter shares everything he/she knows about a strategy, modeling how it works and benefits readers. During the minilesson, observers concentrate on making sense of the demonstration.

When you present minilessons, encourage students to jot down their questions and comments and raise these after the demonstration, though it's okay to allow children to jump in with a question or observation that just can't wait.

In your first minilesson explain the role of observer and presenter, using the following guidelines.

OBSERVER

- 📖 *Listens silently*
- 📖 *Observes carefully*
- 📖 *Notes questions for post-minilesson discussion*

PRESENTER

- 📖 *Prepares demonstration*
- 📖 *Dates chart and identifies strategy*
- 📖 *Models how strategy works*
- 📖 *Thinks out loud*
- 📖 *Connects strategy to own process*
- 📖 *Records key points on chart*

Sparking Insightful Discussions

After the minilesson, I encourage students to ask the presenter any questions they have. Next, I invite students to share ways they use the strategy and record their ideas on the chart. (You'll find that you and your students will add comments to the charts as you return to and review minilessons.) These discussions can expand students' understanding of a strate-

gy, and give them more options to try in their own reading. To stimulate talk, ask questions such as:

- 📖 *What reactions do you have?*
- 📖 *Have you used this strategy? How did it work for you?*
- 📖 *How can the strategy help you as a reader?*
- 📖 *Do you know other ways of solving such a reading problem?*
- 📖 *What suggestions can you add to the list?*

The insights students share during these exchanges are invaluable. After observing a minilesson on rereading that explained how to figure out confusing parts and to recall details, a group of fifth-graders shared their experiences with the strategy. Their comments (below) took rereading way beyond the context of the minilesson:

— I reread parts because they are funny or scary.

— Rereading helps me figure out new words. I look for clues.

— Sometimes the writer tells you the meaning after the word or the situation and that helps me.

— When I reread I tell myself-- concentrate hard so you remember more.

The most memorable comment came from Shauna, who compared rereading to seeing a movie a second time. "The first time you see it," she said, "you just watch for the story. But when you see it again, you can really look at the places, watch the people's actions and what they say. You get in deeper."

Designing a Strategic Reading Minilesson

Because you read, you already know a great deal about reading that can benefit students. To help you plan a minilesson that introduces or clarifies a strategy you and students are working on, ask yourself questions like those below, and jot down notes on a planning sheet (see page 30 for a sample sheet).

📖 *What is the reading strategy?*

📖 *When do I use this strategy?*

📖 *What process do I use?*

📖 *Can I break the process into small parts?*

📖 *Can I find more than one way to demonstrate it?*

📖 *Can I share, with students, any research about the strategy?*

📖 *What book, story, or textbook selection could I use to demonstrate?*

Questions such as these will help you organize your minilesson under headings such as: Why Use?; Process; How The Strategy Can Help; Research; and Notes. As you plan, you can flesh out each section. For example, under "Why Use?" you might plan to point out to kids the reading problem a strategy supports as well as the reasons for using it before, during, or after reading.

Add notes to your planning sheet after the presentation, recording areas you need to clarify, new ideas, students who need extra help, and so forth. My planning sheet for a third-grade minilesson on predicting, along with my post-presentation notes, appears on page 30 (Figure 1).

Collaborating with other teachers to plan minilessons can generate many ideas quickly, as colleagues share how they use the strategy in different grades. Figure 2 shows the planning sheet for a minilesson on questioning that was completed by teachers in Winchester City Schools (see page 31).

Which Minilessons Do I Present?

Minilessons respond to students' needs, and these change throughout the school year. As you reflect on data collected from sources like those listed below, you'll naturally find topics for strategic reading minilessons.

📖 *Strategic Reading Interview*

📖 *Students' Responses to the Seven Questions About Reading*

📖 *Conferences*

📖 *Teacher Observations*

📖 *Reading Strategy Logs*

📖 *Written Work*

📖 *Student Requests*

Whole Class or Small Group Minilessons?

You can present a minilesson to the whole class, small groups, pairs, and even one student. Sometimes a minilesson opens a class; other times you'll interrupt a class to present, repeat, or review one to the whole class or to those who require additional practice.

Minilessons that I prepare in advance, I record on charts prior to presenting. However, the need for a minilesson often arises

A MINILESSON PLANNING SHEET: Predicting

NAME OF STRATEGY	WHY USE
Predicting	to build interest in text
	to assess understanding of text
	to compare reader's ideas with
	what author actually does
	to learn to use text as support
	to learn to distinguish between a guess, support from self, and support from the text

PROCESS	BEFORE, DURING, AFTER
use cover, title,	used throughout process
chapter headings	**before**—limited text knowledge—more a guess and own experiences
use past knowledge	
use text	**during**—move to text and pictures for support—confirm and adjust begin
use illustrations	**after**—make adjustments and use text—confirm or adjust predictions made before reading

HOW IT'S HELPFUL	RESEARCH
involves reader, makes reading active encourages thinking with text	Studies show that good readers predict, confirm, or adjust predictions as they read.
Helps students see when they use past knowledge and/or text	

POST-PRESENTATION NOTES:

Explain difference between right and wrong and confirm or adjust. Need to help them see it's okay to be off target—the point is in the correcting.

Figure 1

MINILESSON PLANNING SHEET

Name of Strategy

. Questioning

Why Use

. to build interest
. to determine prior knowledge
. to focus on the topic
. to use text as support
. to learn new knowledge

Process

. use cover, title, and chapter headings
. use past knowledge
. use text
. use illustrations

Before, During, After

. used throughout process
. before - introduce new vocabulary - develop questions based on cover, title, author, and personal experiences
during - use text and pictures to confirm, adjust, or add to prior knowledge
. after - reread test to support answers - discuss where to find information on unanswered questions - write new knowledge in draft book

How Helpful

. involves reader
. encourages thinking
. makes reading active
. helps students use prior knowledge when reading

Research

. has shown that children need to be taught strategies that will involve them in their reading and writing and will help them solve problems independently. They need to hear how other people think as they handle reading difficulties.

Post Presentation Notes

Patty Ramsey
Kay Hoy
Janice Watkins

Figure 2

in the midst of a guided practice session or during other parts of the day, when you realize that students need an on-the-spot demo. In these cases, you'll still use chart paper to map the minilesson as it proceeds, recording your ideas along with students' comments.

The minilesson on prediction that follows arose after reading third-graders' strategy logs. Twenty out of twenty-two third-graders were unfamiliar with the term *predicting* and wrote, "I don't know."

September 14

MINILESSON: Making Predictions Prior to Reading

[Teacher's Comments: Recorded on Chart Before the Minilesson.]

I always think about the title and front cover of a book, then try to predict or guess what the book will be about. Sometimes I look at pictures inside the book and even read the first page. All good readers make predictions before, during, and after reading. When I think about a book before I read, it's more of a guess, because I haven't read the story. Sometimes I have to change or adjust my prediction after I start to read.

Today, we're going to predict what the picture book, The Hallo-Wiener, will be about, just by thinking about the front cover, the title, and chapter headings.

Have I Used This Strategy? How Did It Work?

— I never do that. I just read.

— I read the back cover or jacket stuff.

— We did that last year. It's fun.

— Our class didn't predict.

Students' Reactions After the Minilesson:

— I got more into the story. I wanted to see what the author did.

— I see the hints in the cover and title now.

— I thought of when I get laughed at and wondered if it would be about that.

— I kept thinking that I want to find out sooner.

Invite Students to Prepare Demonstrations

Students who understand a strategy can present a minilesson to peers who require additional practice. Sixth-grader Paul wrote this in his strategy log after Jeremy's minilesson: "Jeremy showed me how stopping, then summarizing help me remember my science better. He let me watch how he did it and then I did it."

Sixth-graders Tricia, Mark, and Jill planned the minilesson on page 33 and presented it to a small group of classmates who needed extra practice. The notes they prepared reflect their understanding that confirming and adjusting predictions are crucial to comprehension.

MINILESSON : Confirming and Adjusting Predictions

Student-Presenters' Comments: [Recorded Before Demonstration]

It's okay to be off on a prediction. We're off a lot of times. The main part of predicting is you don't have to be right. You can always change your mind and fix your reasons. The part that makes you think is when you change your prediction as you read or after you finish.

The three sixth-graders help students confirm and adjust predictions for the short story, "The Karate Kid" by Gary Soto.

Student-Observers' Comments:

— *It's hard when I have to go back and find stuff. I'm not as fast as my group.*

— *I thought you [Tricia] never had to read it again.*

— *It makes you understand the story more when you got to go back and think about what you said.*

The student-observers' comments convey how powerful it is for students to hear their peers' experiences with the strategies. Reading over the minilesson pinpointed for me that this group needed additional practice skimming and rereading.

Identify students who can present and reinforce strategic reading minilessons. These peer helpers can support students you might not get to that day or week.

Storing Strategic Minilessons

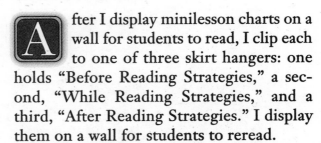 fter I display minilesson charts on a wall for students to read, I clip each to one of three skirt hangers: one holds "Before Reading Strategies," a second, "While Reading Strategies," and a third, "After Reading Strategies." I display them on a wall for students to reread.

I also post a running list of minilessons that includes the date I presented each, so students and I can easily access charts.

Some Closing Thoughts

The minilesson is a type of direct instruction that asks you to do most of your preparation *before* a demonstration. It honors your process and is a way for you to share your wide range of experiences and expertise with others.

Try to spend thirty minutes every other week preparing strategy minilessons with other teachers. Not only is the planning more enjoyable, but, with many heads working together, ideas will develop quickly.

Collaborating with colleagues will enable you to move forward with a strategic reading program. Working as a group provides support, encourages risk taking, and allows us to see that others experience ups and downs and that there is no single, perfect method.

Strategies that Span the Entire Reading Process

This chapter focuses on strategies that readers can use before, while, and after reading: making predictions; asking questions; and the K-W-H-L strategy, an acronym for "What do I Know? What Do I Want to Know? How Will I Find Out?" and "What Have I Learned?"

I've separated my discussion of the strategies into three parts. The first section describes the strategy. The second, "Strategy-In-Action," discusses each strategy's application during minilessons and guided practice. And lastly, the section called "On Their Own," offers ways for students to apply a strategy independently or with peers at any time during the day.

Students will reach independence with these strategies at different points in their school lives. So your goal is not to try to bring everyone up to the same speed, but to help students feel safe enough to risk independent applications, and to emphasize that support from peers and from you is always available to help them through those bumpy, unsure moments.

Whether you are demonstrating through a minilesson or involving students in guided practice, always refer to the strategy by its name. This way, students will be able to call upon specific strategies as they monitor reading and the need arises to solve problems independently.

Making Predictions

Book Selection: Pause for a moment and think about how you choose a book. For vacation and entertainment reading, you might select what I call a fast, easy read with lots of action, romance, and perhaps mystery. At other times you might choose to reread a favorite nineteenth-century novel, or read a series of books in your favorite genre. When you and I read for pleasure, we choose books that won't frustrate or cause us to struggle. When we select books that we expect will please us, we are using prediction strategies. Predicting begins when readers look for a book that they *might* enjoy and can read with fluency.

If readers select books that are way beyond their ability, they may check books out, look at the illustrations or photographs, but not read or enjoy the text. These students will begin to develop competency and find pleasure in reading if they read at their comfort level. Developing predicting strategies will help children find choice reading they can enjoy at their comfort level. After all, free-choice reading should be fun, pleasurable, and entertaining. Children need the same opportunities for choices as adults, especially if they are to develop reading tastes and learn what kinds of books they enjoy.

STRATEGY-IN-ACTION:
Book Selection

The following suggestions can help students predict whether or not they will enjoy a book.

- 📖 *Look at the title and cover. Read the back cover or summary inside the book's jacket.*

- 📖 *Browse through the illustrations or photographs.*

- 📖 *Read the chapter headings or Table of Contents.*

- 📖 *Ask friends, your teacher, and librarian for recommendations.*

- 📖 *Find books about your hobbies or favorite topics.*

- 📖 *Look for other books by an author/illustrator you enjoyed.*

> **Teach students who are reading chapter books the five-finger method of determining if a book is too hard: Ask them to turn to any page and begin reading. If there are five words they can't pronounce or don't understand, then the book is too difficult.**

Adapt the five finger method to the needs of beginning readers by making it the two-or the three-finger method, and have them choose another book if they can't pronounce or don't understand two or three words on a page.

Some students will want to check the book out anyway. Let them, and then suggest that they ask someone at home to read it aloud, or ask an older reading buddy at school. You might even read the book aloud to the entire class!

Predicting Before and While Reading: In addition to creating anticipation, predicting before reading can activate learners' prior knowledge and experiences about a topic. Recall and comprehension can improve when readers think about what they know about a topic before they even open the front cover of the book.

As good readers move further into a story, they continue to predict and support, confirm or adjust their hunches as the narrative unfolds. In fact, predictions become more logical as readers collect information from the text and think about their hunches. "If I can't adjust a prediction," observed second-grader Sage, "then I need to reread because I didn't get it."

Work with the entire class and model how making predictions works before and during reading. Record their responses on large chart paper. By observing and experiencing how predicting can involve readers in the story, reluctant learners might risk trying the strategy.

The description of the Predict-and-Support Strategy that follows illustrates how third-graders used predicting to think about the story.

STRATEGY-IN-ACTION: Predict and Support

During a minilesson, introduce a prediction chart as a framework for organizing thinking and helping students sort out whether predictions come from clues in the text or their own experiences. The chart consists of three headings: *Predictions, Support, Based On* (see page 38).

Students and I complete several prediction charts during guided practice; they observe how predicting works before and while reading.

I use picture books for these sessions, as it is possible to complete a chart during one guided practice session.

Stop once or twice during the reading and invite students to predict. Do not adjust predictions at this point, but wait until you've completed the book. Stopping to analyze can disrupt the movement of the story to a point that causes students to lose interest. Moreover, you want to observe whether or not the predictions students make during reading reflect their growing knowledge of the text and illustrations.

Before reading—and each time I pause in the text—I tell the class that I'll take two to three predictions. I also explain that over a period of two to three weeks, everyone will have had a turn. On my clipboard, I keep a class roster and note who has contributed, marking the date next to each name. Setting a limit on contributions beforehand also moves the lesson along.

Predicting Practice Using *The Hallo-Wiener*

Twenty-two third graders gather around the chart stand to practice predicting with Dav Pilkey's *The Hallo-Wiener*. The demonstration opens with a question: "Can you predict what this story will be about?"

Figure 1

Students study the cover (Figure 1). Two children use clues from the illustration, and point out elements in the cover as support (Figure 2[1]). Nina, however, predicts the story will be about name-calling. When I ask her why she thinks this, she says that her older brother calls her, "niner-wiener."

Encourage children to explain their predictions with questions such as: What made you say that? Can you tell me why you said that? Students' predictions can be based on the text, illustrations, their own experiences, peers' comments, or a combination of all four. The ability to identify where support comes from is part of thinking and moving to valid interpretations.

The Hallo-Wiener   by Dav Pilkey

Predictions Before Reading	Support	Based On
It's about a dog who likes hot dogs - other dogs tease him. It's about a dog who looks like a hot dog.	The dog looks sad. Other dogs point at him and laugh.	The picture on the front cover. The word "wiener" in the title means hot dog.
A dog dresses up like a hot dog for Halloween. Other dogs make fun of him.	The hot dog on the cover. The dog alone behind it. Others laugh. Hallo-wiener sounds like Halloween	Words in the title. Picture on the cover.
It's about name calling. The dog behind the hot dog is sad because he's called names. It said "Oscar did not like it one bit." He was more angry than sad.	My brother calls me "niner the wiener." That's what will happen in this book.	What happened to me and how I felt.

Figure 2 [1]

The Hallo-Wiener   by Dav Pilkey

Predictions Stop #1	Support	Based On
The costume will be a hot dog costume.	• Hot dog on cover. • Shape of the box. • Oscar almost fainted when he looked in the box. • His mom lovingly calls Oscar a Vienna sausage and sausage link. • Other dogs laugh at Oscar and call him "Wiener dog."	The cover picture. The picture of the box. Parts of the story.
Stop #2 Oscar knows it's not a monster.	• He sees paws and tail sticking out.	Picture on dock. Oscar saw what others didn't see.
Oscar will save the dogs, but I hope he won't. The others shared their candy. They changed his nickname from "Wiener Dog" to "Hero Sandwich." Oscar had friends. No one made fun of him again.	• Oscar was never mean. • Oscar wanted friends - if he saves them, maybe they'll like Oscar. • Oscar tries to keep up with others even though they make fun of him - shows he wants to be friends.	Oscar's nice - he wore the costume to keep his mom happy. Oscar is not afraid - he checks monster out.

Figure 2 [2]

In the first stop I make while reading *The Hallo-Wiener*, I invite students to predict what kind of costume Oscar's mother has made for him. Students' reasons (see Figure 2[2]) are based on the cover, the shape of the box that holds the costume, and Mother's comment, "Happy Halloween, my little sausage link."

When Oscar shows up on the dock, I pause and ask: "What will Oscar do?" Here students use the clues in the illustration and, like Oscar, conclude that the monster is a "couple of ornery cats." But many also voice their feelings about fairness and Oscar's so-called friends "getting what they deserve."

Josh predicts that Oscar will not rescue the dogs struggling in the pond. "I would get back on anyone who was as mean as those dogs were to Oscar." Amanda counters with, "That's how *you* feel. But I think the story shows that Oscar wants friends so badly that he will find a way to help them and show what a friend he [Oscar] is." The tensions that arise in conversations that result from predicting help students think deeply about a story. And as Amanda said, "It's fun because you never know if you're thinking like the author until you read the whole book."

On Their Own

Continue to devote guided practice sessions to the Predict-and-Support Strategy, until you sense students can work independently. Then, during guided practice, invite students to practice this strategy on their own with the following activity.

For this activity I often use short stories and folk tales that have two to three places ideal for students to pause and predict. First I divide the story into two or three parts and give students one part at a time to read. This prevents reading ahead and also encourages students to use what they have read to predict and find evidence. After reading each section, students complete a prediction chart (Figure 3[1]). Sometimes groups share their charts with one another; at other times several students share with the entire class. Younger children can discuss their adjustments, older students can write these (Figure 3[2]).

Because some students have so much to write, they can record their "predictions," "support," and "based on" in a paragraph. Continue guided practice with students who need it.

I keep a file of stories, culling them from *Storyworks* and *Cricket* magazines, and from collections of stories such as Alvin Schwartz's *Stories to tell A Cat; Short and Shivery*, edited by Robert Sans Souci; or

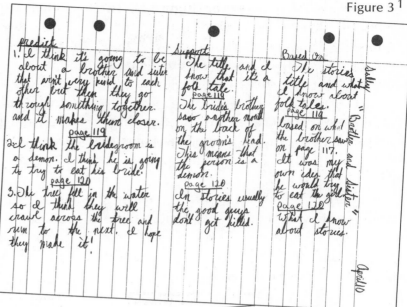

Figure 3[1]

Figure 3[2]

In a guided practice lesson using "Brother and Sister," an African folk tale, Sally predicts, supports, and then adjusts her prediction.

American Tall Tales retold by Mary Pope Osborne. Exchange stories for guided reading with colleagues. This way you enlarge your choices and save valuable time searching for appropriate titles.

Analyzing Predictions After Reading:

Now readers return to the predictions made before and while reading to confirm or adjust them.

Making adjustments after reading requires analyzing a hunch in relation to the actual story. Students quickly observe that early predictions are frequently off-target because the reader depends more on personal experience rather than the text.

STRATEGY-IN-ACTION: Confirm or Adjust Predictions

Model rereading and scanning the pictures in a book you've just finished to help find supportive facts and inferences. After finishing a story with the class, invite students to return to the prediction chart to confirm and adjust their ideas. (I write the adjustments students make on the chart with a different color marker pen so they can easily compare initial predictions with what actually occurred in the story.)

On Their Own

Predicting with a Partner: Pair students up whenever they visit the classroom or school library to check out books. Students listen to one another's predictions and then help each other with the five-, two- or three-finger method.

Invite children to suggest ways to adapt this—and other—peer support ideas. For example, a group of third-graders wanted to switch partners each month. "We could choose one time and you the next," they said. It was a great idea, and so that's exactly what happened.

Read-Pause-Predict: Students can practice Read-Pause-Predict with a partner after you and a student have modeled the process for the class.

Using the same picture book or novel chapter, partners agree, prior to reading, to stop at a certain point, then predict. Pairs share predictions, offer support, then continue reading to confirm or adjust their predictions.

Each student is responsible for encouraging his or her partner to provide support from the text. Teach students helpful questions such as:

Can you show me where in the story you got that idea? Can you tell me what happened in the story that supports your idea?

Prediction Book Reports: Traditional book-reports too often turn out to be nothing more than a retelling. In order to invite a more meaningful response, I like to offer students a framework for book reporting that integrates the entire process of making predictions.

Prediction Book Report Framework:

1 Study the cover illustrations. Read the title and first page. Predict what the book will be about. Provide support and explain where you found that support.

2 After reading the first two chapters, predict what will happen, using what you've read to support your ideas. (In an easy reader or picture book, stop after the first two to three pages.)

3 Stop before reading the last chapter. Predict the outcome and offer specific reasons from the story to support your theory.

4 Now that you've completed the book, reread all of your predictions. Make adjustments by writing above a sentence or in the margin.

Fifth-grader Jaime's report on Patricia MacLachlan's *Baby* illustrates how well she applies all aspects of predicting (Figures 4¹–4³).

Pairs or small groups of students can discuss a book using the four steps. Here, students adjust their predictions as they read and stop, because the emphasis is on talking, not writing and then rethinking.

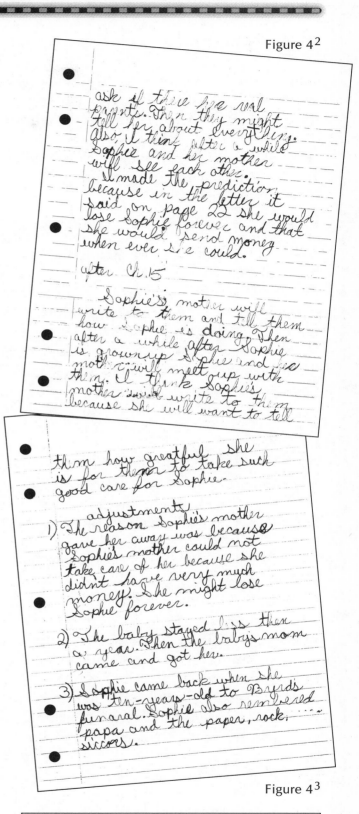

Figure 4²

ask if there are real parents. Then they might tell her about everything. Also, I think after a while Sophie and her mother will see each other. I made the prediction because in the letter it said on page 22 she would lose Sophie forever and that she would send money when ever she could.

after Ch. 15

Sophie's mother will write to them and tell them how Sophie is doing. Then after a while after Sophie is grownup Sophie and his mother will meet up with them. I think Sophie's mother will write to them because she will want to tell

them how greatful she is for them to take such good care for Sophie.

adjustments
1) The reason Sophie's mother gave her away was because Sophie's mother could not take care of her because she didn't have very much money. She might lose Sophie forever.

2) The baby stayed less then a year. Then the babys mom came and got her.

3) Sophie came back when she was ten-years-old to Byrds funaral. Sophie also remembered papa and the paper, rock, sicors.

Figure 4³

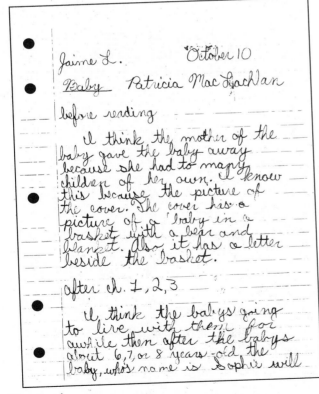

Jaime L.   October 10

Baby   Patricia MacLachlan

before reading

I think the mother of the baby gave the baby away because she had to many children of her own. I know this because the picture of the cover. The cover has a picture of a baby in a basket with a bear and blanket. Also it has a letter beside the basket.

after ch. 1, 2, 3

I think the babys going to live with them for awhile then after the babys about 6,7,or 8 years-old the baby, who's name is Sophie will

Figure 4¹

Fifth-grader Jaime's independent prediction book report and adjustments.

Reading Logs: At the back of a reading response journal or a reading folder, have students list the free-choice books they have completed. Such records honor independent reading, enable you and students to discuss the types of books students have selected, the number of books they've read, and favorite authors and illustrators.

Posing Questions

Asking Questions Before Reading: Posing questions before reading fiction, nonfiction, or a textbook chapter encourages students to set purposes for reading. The questions also provide students with a framework for thinking as they read and helps them monitor their ability to remember information.

STRATEGY-IN-ACTION: Browse and Question

Browsing can bond children to the contents of a book, create an interest in the book, and build a desire to read. Browsing invites children to look at a book's covers and end papers; the illustrations, photographs, charts, or graphs, captions, headings, chapter titles, and words in boldface.

Demonstrating how to browse is a worthwhile minilesson. Browsing stimulates curiosity and an abundance of questions and can generate enthusiasm for fiction, nonfiction, magazines, and even a textbook chapter. Fifth grader Jason's questions arose after he scanned the first four chapters of Jim Haskin's *Get On Board: The Story of the Underground Railroad* (Figure 5).

Asking Questions While Reading: The questions raised before reading can move readers into a book and generate enthusi-

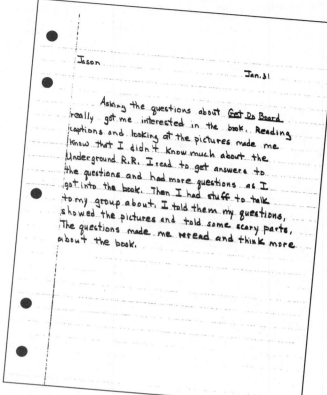

Figure 5

Jason's self-evaluation for asking questions before reading helps him understand how the strategy helped.

Jason's work illustrates a benefit of browsing: Developing a reason for reading the book. (Best of all, the motivation came from Jason.)

asm for completing the book.

Invite students to work in small **groups** or as partners. Have them pose and discuss questions after reading the first two **or three** chapters of a novel. A group of **third** graders read up to chapter 3 of *Lily and Miss Liberty* by Carla Stevens, and then jotted down one or two questions in their strategy logs before discussing them.

— Why is the chapter called "Fourteen Crowns?"

— Why does Lily want money for the Pedestal Fund?

— Is Lily going to get enough money to take to school?

— Will anyone help Lily get the money?

Part of the third-graders' conversation is shown below. I think it illustrates how questions raised while reading chapter books can stimulate additional predictions—and deepen students' commitment to a story.

Heather: We all asked about the title. I think she'll make fourteen crowns because of the cover.

Justin: I think she'll make the crowns, but who would buy something a kid made?

Amanda: Her [Lily's] mom won't help her because she's against the pedestal fund.

Lily and Miss Liberty
by CARLA STEVENS
illustrated by DEBORAH KOGAN RAY

Heather: Maybe her father or grandma will help.

Amanda: Lily's got to get money. I hope she does.

Justin: Her friends have jobs. But there's nothing left for her.

Their questions and discussion reveal that they can use what they know about Lily to predict, and that they have a good handle on the story.

STRATEGY-IN-ACTION: Questions that Monitor Understanding

Sometimes readers bump into passages and words that confuse. They need strategies that identify confusing parts, so they can help themselves or seek support.

Help students ask themselves questions that check their comprehension, such as: Does this passage make sense? Are there words that confuse me? Can I pronounce all the words? How much do I recall? These questions help readers pinpoint confusing sections in a book.

To demonstrate this strategy, transcribe a passage that confused you from a book onto chart paper or an overhead transparency. Point to the difficult words and phrases. Model how you are unable to retell the passage in your own words. Show students how you looked for context clues in the passage, in the sections before and after the passage, and then reread to understand.

Asking Questions After Reading: In addition to raising discussion and study questions, have students return to the list of questions they posed before starting a book. Read through the list, noting questions the text did and did not answer. Point out that good readers seek out other books to find explanations for unanswered questions

Lily and Miss Liberty, for example, raised many questions about the Statue of Liberty in Amanda's mind. She volunteered to collect additional information and proudly read her report to classmates (Figure 6).

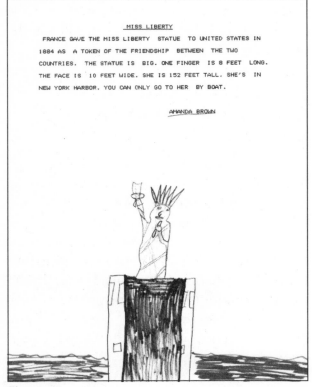

Figure 6

STRATEGY-IN-ACTION: Questions That Encourage Personal Connections

Connecting with the lives and experiences of fictional and biographical characters powerfully bonds readers and books. When readers tell me they dream about a character, draw pictures of favorite characters and places, and act out parts of the story, I know they entered the characters' lives. Cultivating this connection is one of the most important reading strategies of all.

Sometimes that personal connection draws a student into reading. For Keysha, a reluctant reader, Katherine Paterson's *The Great Gilly Hopkins* swept her away and helped her sort out her own experience of loss. In a letter to Gilly's mother, Keysha wrote, "I know how Gilly feels. My momma left me last year and I cried and cried myself to sleep. Can't you see that Gilly and I need mothers?" Keysha reread the book, then asked me, "Got any others like that one?" And I handed her *The Pinballs* by Betsy Byars.

Pairs or small groups of students can discuss the questions below that foster personal connections. I put each question on an index card to form a card deck of questions. Students can select a card to discuss or you can make several decks and give one to each group.

Is there a passage in the story you found meaningful? Read it and explain why.

Have you had any experiences that are similar to those of a character in the story?

How did the story make you feel? Can you explain what about the story aroused these feelings?

Is there a character in the story you relate to? What do you both have in common?

Did this story change or affect your beliefs about life? people? Explain.

On Their Own

Writing Open-Ended Questions: To write thought-provoking questions requires a thorough knowledge of the text and the ability to "think along" with the story or information.

Teach students to write questions that help them discover the implied meanings in the story. Set a standard for valid interpretations by calling for two to three pieces of evidence. Model how you can "test" a question to see if it goes beyond the facts. For example, in *The Hallo-Wiener*, I had students answer both questions below, then discuss the difference between them:

1 What kind of costume does Oscar wear? How do Oscar's friends react to his costume?

2 Why does Oscar save the friends who make fun of him?

The chart third-graders created (below) analyzes both questions.

When we reviewed the chart, Heather and Tim explained the difference between the two questions this way: "There was only one way to answer number one, but lots of ways to answer number two. We used lots of different reasons for number two." They all agreed that it took longer to figure out number two, "because we had to go deeper and deeper into it [the story]."

Sometimes, when groups of students discuss questions they have raised about the setting, plot, theme, or characters in a book, I have them use a strip of paper, to mark the part in the book they used to prove their interpretation. Such support can be factual, or logical inferences drawn from the facts.

Question Guides for Nonfiction: Questions raised by students before they read assigned pages in a textbook or an informational book serve several purposes:

📖 *They create a reason for reading.*

📖 *They encourage investment in the book.*

📖 *They stimulate discussions about the book.*

📖 *They can serve as a review sheet for a quiz.*

Help students to make question guides using the six steps shown below and on page 46, though it's a good idea to do it as a class first.

1 Skim the assigned sections by reading bold-faced headings; captions for pictures, charts, and graphs; and

Number 1	Number 2
a hot dog outfit	It says Oscar was a "true friend"
They laugh and make fun of him and call him "Wiener Dog"	A "true friend" helps others
	Oscar turns his costume into a raft and saves them from drowning because he's a caring person—he even wore the costume because his mom made it for him—and did not take it off when others laughed at him
	Oscar wants friends and sees this as a chance to get some

vocabulary written in boldface.

2 Fold notebook paper in half, lengthwise.

3 Write the heading "Questions" on the left-hand side. On the right-hand side, write the heading "Notes."

4 Formulate questions that previewing raises—questions that focus on the new information presented in these pages.

5 Leave space between questions so you can fill in after reading. This will leave room for notes collected during class discussions.

6 Record notes on the right-hand side, opposite questions and under the "Notes" heading.

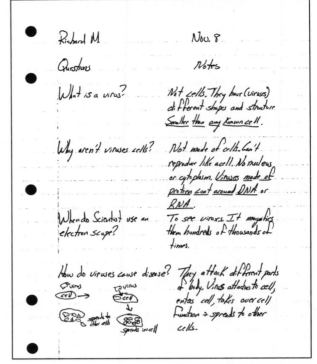

Figure 8   *Sixth-graders' question guide*

The question guide shown here (Figure 8) is based on a sixth-grade science text about viruses. Notice how the student separates independent work from class work by underlining the notes added during discussion.

Discussion Highlights: I find it impossible to monitor six simultaneous book discussions. So during a 45-minute class, I join one or two groups and listen to the conversations generated by students' questions. I ask students to be prepared to wrap up their discussions about ten minutes before the class ends. During these last ten minutes, students summarize, in journals, the highlights of their group's discussion. Each student includes points she or he made, ideas offered by others, and conflicting issues.

You can read these summaries yourself, or begin the next class by inviting students to share them. The journal entry on page 47, written by a sixth-grader after her group discussed Katherine Paterson's *The Tale of the Mandarin Ducks*, illustrates how effectively these summaries can capture the essence of the talks. (The group had selected a quote from the story to discuss.)

The K-W-H-L

This strategy, developed by researcher Donna Ogle, was originally called the K-W-L—shorthand for three questions designed to engage readers in nonfiction texts: What do I know? What do I want to know? What have I learned? The questions elicit children's prior knowledge, pique their curiosity about a topic, and support research, motivating students to seek answers for their questions in other texts.

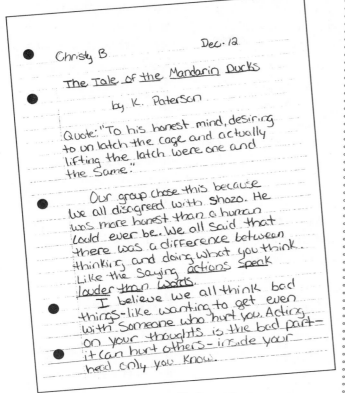

Figure 9

Sixth-grader's summary of group discussion

Recently, teachers have added the "H" so that students engaged in research can also consider, How Will I Go About Learning? The question compels students to think of information-gathering ideas such as: interview an expert, plan a survey, browse through newspapers, take photographs, conduct an experiment, ask the librarian for help.

Before Reading: Using a fast write, students discover what they already know and feel about a topic. Allow several minutes for students to write their ideas without censoring any thoughts. Point out that they can confirm and adjust these after completing research.

STRATEGY-IN-ACTION: Fast Write

This strategy works best for students who can write fluently. Have students write a paragraph that is a free outpouring of what they already know about a subject. Students keep writing, even if they have to repeat a word until a new idea surfaces (Figure 9[1] below and Figure 9[2], page 48).

STRATEGY-IN-ACTION: What Do I Want to Know?

Students skim their textbook's or browse through library books and magazines. They then compose a list of questions and statements that express what they would like to learn. Such a list creates a desire to read and research. It also helps students focus on specific aspects of a topic as they read.

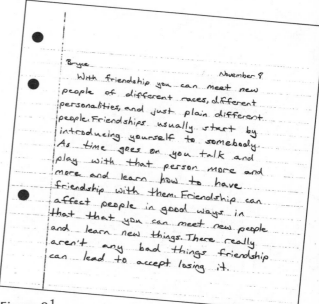

Figure 9[1]

Sixth-grader's fast write on friendship. Completed before reading Mildred Taylor's The Friendship.

Figure 9² — *Fifth-grader's fast write before investigating volcanoes.*

> Sally   December 16
>   Fast Write Volcanos
>   They exsisted about the
> time when the dinosoures were
> on the earth. They are still
> here today but they don't
> erupt any more. They are
> still very hot inside though.
>   People can not go near
> valcanos so scientists have
> made robots to go in or
> on valcanos to take pictures.
> Valcanos are not here in
> America but there are ones
> in Hawaii and other places.
> The ocean has covered many
> up, I think.

Figure 10¹ — *Fourth-grader's K-W-L guided practice using* Banshee *by Virginia Hamilton.*

> Banshee   May 15
> 11. Laura Horton
>   What I know about Banshee:
> I do not know what Banshees
> are, but I think they might be
> a tribe.
>
>   What Would I like to know
> about Banshee:
> Where do they(it, the?) live?
> What do they(it, the?) wear?
> What do they(it, the?) eat?
> What do they(it, the?) look like?
>
>   What I have learned:
> The Banshee is a woman who
> represents death. She has long
> hair and wears a cloak. She
> screams. She is deaths announcer,
> She looks deadly.

Figure 10² — *Laura's visualization of a Banshee.*

After Reading: Students can demonstrate what they learned through informal discussions and journal entries. Ideas for more formal oral presentations and projects can come from students or from a list prepared by students and teacher. Journal entries, projects, and presentations can be used to assess what students have learned.

Fourth-grader Laura practices the KWL in her strategy log (Figure 10¹). When we discussed this entry, Laura said, "I couldn't wait to read about Banshees after I saw I didn't know much. I even drew a picture" (Figures 10²).

Some Closing Thoughts

The predicting strategy is one of the most important reading and thinking strategies. It's the one I focused on the first year I implemented strategic reading instruction. Predicting is a complex strategy that includes many other reading strategies. To predict, readers question and wonder, then read on to confirm or adjust. The process of confirming and adjusting involves finding support in the text. To find support learners reread to recall facts and make inferences. Moreover, predictions foster the motivation to read on and reread, encouraging an inner dialogue between readers and writer.

If you're wondering where to begin your strategic reading program, start with predictions—you'll be doing much more than asking, "What will happen next?"

Strategies to Use During and After Reading

— "If I don't understand pages I skip them. Sometimes I skip over three pages. I never go back." *Grade 4*

— "Sometimes I'm in the middle of a book and don't understand stuff. So I put the book back" *Grade 3*

— "I just read what's on the page and write the titles and authors in my log. Don't ask me to think or talk about them." *Grade 6*

Needless to say, comments like these concern me. It's disheartening to see students going through the motions of reading and identifying confusing parts, and yet lacking a deep involvement with books and strategies to help them cope with parts of books that seem difficult. These are the things I want to help them develop.

This chapter presents additional strategies that students can use during and after reading to help make reading more meaningful. These strategies encourage reflection, offer ways for learners to deal with confusing passages in texts, and continue to connect students to characters' lives and new information.

Reading Rate

Fifth-grader Katee had difficulty recalling what she had read during class time. When I asked her to write why she didn't remember chunks of text, she revealed a feeling that many children have (Figure 1, page 52).

Katee's belief that finishing fast is the mark of a good reader is all too common. You can alleviate kids' anxiety about this by

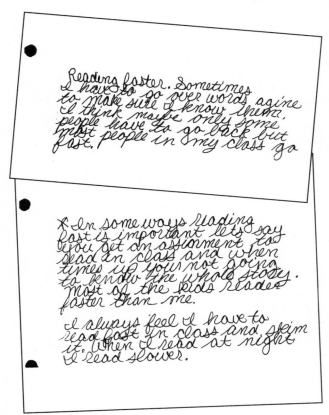

Reading faster. Sometimes
I have to go over words agine
to make sure I know them.
I think maybe only some
people have to go back but
most people in my class go
fast.

X In some ways reading
fast is important lets say
you get an assignment to
read in class and when
times up your not going
to know the whole story.
Most of the kids reades
faster than me.

I always feel I have to
read fast in class and skim
it. When I read at night
I read slower.

Figure 1

explaining that everyone in the group will finish at different times. Always allow enough time for all students to finish.

Offer choices to students who complete their reading earlier; this will maintain the quiet other classmates need to finish their reading.

Or, invite the faster readers to reread, read their library book, write a reaction in a journal, or raise questions for discussion.

STRATEGY-IN-ACTION:
Adjusting Reading Rates

Develop minilessons to help students understand when to change their reading rate. When reading to remember, slow down to savor and enjoy words, images, illustrations, events and dialogue. Slow down to absorb new information and think about it as you read.

After students read, suggest they practice skimming to locate support in the text to prove a position, discuss issues and questions. Show students how to skim a page for key words, phrases, a character's name, or bold-face section headings. Point out how much faster skimming is than reading to remember and understand. Skimming is a short-term memory activity; slowing down and thinking about the text can place information in long-term memory.

Rereading

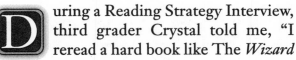uring a Reading Strategy Interview, third grader Crystal told me, "I reread a hard book like The *Wizard of Oz* three times. I do it over and over until I understand and the reading is easier." Good readers seem to figure out the benefits of rereading.

In the same third-grade class, Cal told me, "I never reread. Only dumb kids reread." Before modeling and practicing strategies that incorporate rereading, I ask the class to work in small groups and talk about rereading. My goal is to get kids to view rereading as a positive habit. The strategy fosters reading fluency, better recall of details, improved word recognition. Ultimately it builds students' self-confidence. After the third-graders talked, they wrote their ideas on chart paper:

How Rereading Can Help You

— Understand hard words.

— Find things you did not find before.

— Help the story make sense.

— Make it more interesting.

— Help you memorize if you need to for a contest.

— Make you a better reader.

— Find words and sentences you skipped.

— Keep reading a part over and you'll get it.

— Make reading more fun because you go over the best parts.

A pretty terrific list! The strategies that follow also invite students to reread in order to support comprehension during and after reading.

STRATEGY-IN-ACTION: Pause-Think-Retell

Encourage children to pause after each chapter; once or twice during a picture book; and after each section of a textbook. Show them how you stop, think, and then retell in order to monitor how much you recall. Point out that thinking and retelling reinforces remembering the text. If there is little recall, then reread and try to retell again.

Many students read and have little or no recall. This can be due to an inability to concentrate, to a lack of prior knowledge, or because the vocabulary is too difficult. If after two rereadings the passage still confuses, then students should seek assistance from a peer or the teacher.

Retelling

R etelling entire stories is an excellent way for students to monitor how much they remember. The point is not to memorize the exact words, but for a child to recall in his/her own words, details about character, setting, plot, dialogue, or information. When monitoring oral and written retellings, look for the following:

SETTING

📖 Student can tell where and when the story takes place.

CHARACTERS AND PROBLEMS

📖 Names main character and problems he/she faced.

📖 Names other characters and shows how these connect to main character.

PLOT

📖 Recalls the important events.

📖 Sequences the events.

📖 Includes rich details

📖 Includes beginning/middle/end of story.

📖 Demonstrates an understanding of concepts and information.

SOLUTION

📖 Shows how problems were solved.

PERSONAL CONNECTIONS

📖 Offers feelings and reactions.

📖 Makes connections between characters and events and own life.

PRESENTATION

📖 Speaks fluently.

📖 Uses vocabulary from text.

STRATEGY-IN-ACTION:
Multiple Readings and Written Retellings

Students can write and self-evaluate multiple retellings of the same story or nonfiction book. Invite them to read the story or part of the nonfiction text once and retell it. On each of the next two days, have students reread and retell the same text, then draw conclusions about their retellings.

Fourth-grader Sally understands the power of revisiting a challenging book after two rereadings and retellings of a section from *African Journey* by John G. Chiasson. Her ability to recall more and more details after each reading led Sally to a deeper understanding of the benefits of multiple readings (Figures 2¹–2³).

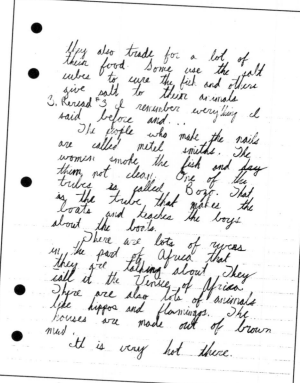

Figure 2 ²

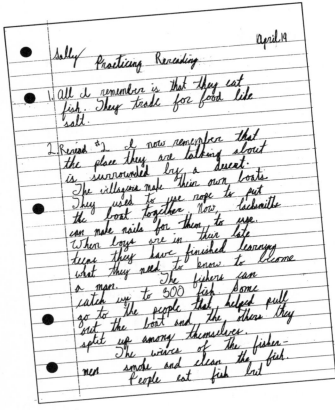

Figure 2 ¹

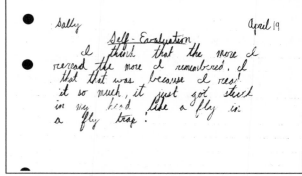

Figure 2 ³

Figures 2 ¹, 2 ², and 2 ³ are from Sally's Strategy Log: Practice Rereading and Remembering.

STRATEGY-IN-ACTION:
Lists As Retellings

Retellings of sections and/or chapters from science and social studies textbooks can be in list form. Students write a list of the causes of the Revolutionary War, a list of crafts made and sold in the colonies, or a list of the conditions that make up weather. Lists can help focus students on significant parts of a chapter.

With literature, students can make lists of things characters value or dislike; problems characters face; the different settings in a story; or the important events in a chapter, short story, or entire novel.

Fifth-grader Sally's list of what Sarah values, in *Sarah Plain and Tall*, and sixth-grader Bobby's list of emotions characters felt in Chapter 4 of Betsy Byar's *The Pinballs* (Figures 3 & 4) illustrate how retelling can be elevated to thinking when students reread to select specific information.

Sally found examples from the story to support her ideas (Figure 5). Bobby used his list as a guide during a group discussion. Bobby's self-evaluation (Figure 6, page 56) explains why the list was helpful.

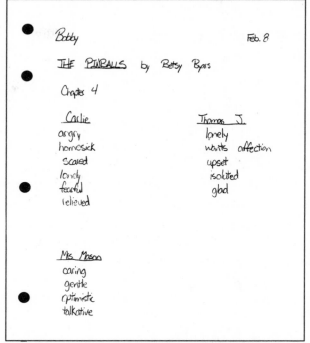

Figure 4   *Bobby's list of characters' emotions from Chapter 4 of* The Pinballs.

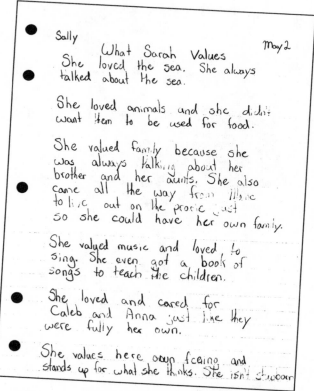

Figure 5   *Sally's items from the story that support each item on her list.*

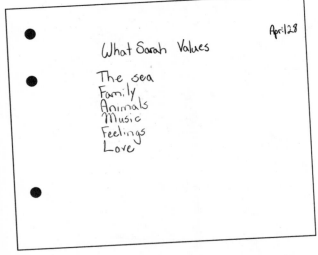

Figure 3   *By Sally*

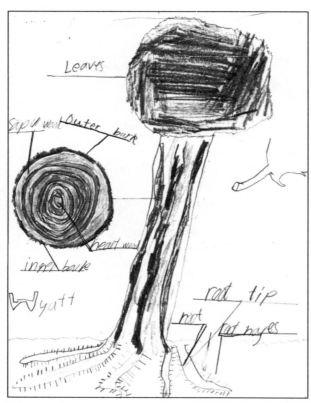

Figure 6   *Bobby's evaluation of how his list helped him discuss Chapter 4 with his group.*

Figure 7 [1]

Figures 7 [1], 7 [2], and 7 [3]—Wyatt's double entry on trees.

STRATEGY-IN-ACTION: Double Entry Journals

Double entry journals can help students retell content area information. Students set up their journal so that the left hand side is for a diagram, pictures, a map, or chart; the right hand side is for retelling. For example, a labeled diagram of the heart on the left-hand side becomes a guide for explaining how the heart pumps blood to the lungs and the body. Such retellings make excellent study guides for tests and quizzes.

The double entry on the parts of a tree by third grader Wyatt (Figures 7 [1], 7 [2] and 7 [3]), and the double entry by fourth-grader Bryce, (Figures 8 [1], 8 [2], page 57) illustrate how retelling and explaining can help students learn complicated information. To complete the entry, both boys had to "reread to get all the facts."

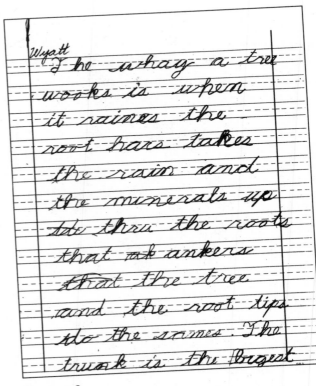

Figure 7 [2]

part of the tree. Than the minerals and stuf gous thru the sap wood. Then minerals and rain go through the branches of the tree and into the leaves. Light

Figure 7 [3]

Rereading to Connect, Infer, and Draw Conclusions

When you provide experiences after reading that invite students to skim or reread parts of a text, you help students interpret a story and analyze information. The strategies that follow move students deeper into texts by inviting them to make connections to past experiences and knowledge, draw conclusions, and create new understandings.

STRATEGY-IN-ACTION: The Think-Aloud

The think-aloud asks students to verbalize their thoughts, questions, and connections as they read a text line by line. Model the process with a student-partner. Show how students can work together to understand confusing words or phrases. Though both

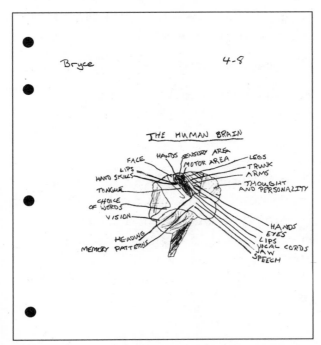

Figure 8 [1]   *Bryce's double entry on the brain.*

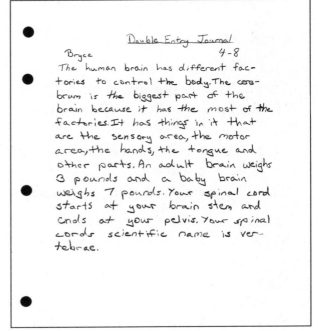

Figure 8 [2]

students can ask questions, it is the peer helper's responsibility to ask probing questions of the student who needs support.

Sample Think-Aloud

The following think-aloud is based on the opening eight lines of Shonto Begay's poem, "Our Mysteries, His Knowledge." James and Kayla, two sixth-graders, have read the poem many times. James had the background knowledge to help Kayla understand the images and connect to the poem.

Our Mysteries, His Knowledge

That which we can only guess to be
    Like voiceless vacant villages of old
    Coyote, Ma'ii, was always there to see
    What the rest of us are only told.

Like pictographs, like broken pottery shards
    We have yet to see this picture whole
    A timeless creature keeping constant
      guard
    Of what he's seen while playing his
      many roles.

He's seen diaspora centuries before
    His fur forever ruffled, his senses wide
      awake
    While watching life and death from his
      vermillion ledge
    Since the great wind, since the quake.

When Anasazi villages were cleared
    Before his eyes like secrets carved in
      stone
    He heard silence fall on mesas far and
      near
    Now the mysteries of our lives are his
      alone.

Transcription of Think-Aloud

K: Line 2 talks about the past that can't talk anymore—like the dead. Line 3 tells how coyote sees all from the past. Line 4 says that we learn about the past from stories. Like when my grandma tells me what was it like when she grew up in Georgia.

J: What about the first line?

K: I don't know.

J: Why does he [Shonto Begay] use "guess?"

K: Maybe because we never know for sure how things were before we lived. What are pictographs and shards [line 5]?

J: Shards are pieces of pottery that archaeologists dig up and pictographs are pictures that mean things, like the hieroglyphics in ancient Egypt.

K: Maybe he says those words because they are from the past like the stories. But we can't understand the past I think that's what he means in lines 6.

J: What does *timeless* do to coyote?

K: Maybe he [Begay] is saying that coyote is like a spirit that is forever and people aren't.

In the brief conference that followed the think-aloud, Kayla told me that she loved the sound of this poem. "I say it a lot and even copied it in my log," she explained, "but some of the words I didn't know." Working with James helped Kayla enter into the very heart of the poem.

STRATEGY-IN-ACTION: Making Inferences

Children make inferences in daily life. Help make students aware of how much they draw conclusions based on the talk and actions of family members, peers, etc.

Mini-dramas build a bridge between inferences children make each day and inferences they can make from books. Create situations that students can dramatize for the class, and then invite the audience to infer and draw conclusions. The partial list of possible situations below can be used as mini-dramas that allow students to observe and discover a range of possible inferences or implied meanings. Make these statements to students, and then ask what inferences they'd draw if:

- *A student yawns several times.*
- *Two students pass notes to one another.*
- *A student falls asleep.*
- *One student takes a pen from a classmate's desk.*
- *Two students argue over who gets the soccer ball.*
- *A group of students has not completed homework.*
- *A group of students copies homework from one student.*
- *Three students leave the room without permission.*
- *A student returns from recess crying.*
- *Two students left all their books at home.*

Daily school events will provide you with dozens of other situations.

I like to put each mini-drama on an index card, then have students choose one to present. Once children demonstrate an ease with expressing implied meanings during mini-dramas, move them to literature.

Talking to Infer and Draw Conclusions

Third graders reading *Lily and Miss Liberty* discuss the feelings Lily experienced in Chapter 5. Heather rereads this paragraph from page 35:

> When Miss Pearson called on Lily, Lily's heart gave a flutter. She unpinned the little purse from her dress, opened it, and let the money fall into her hand. Then she walked up the aisle and handed it to Miss Pearson. "Ninety-five cents," she said.

Five students talk about the passage because talking helps readers draw lots of diverse meanings from a short passage. The range of ideas generated illustrates the high level of thinking children have achieved. Note how students use words from the paragraph and parts of the story to back up ideas.

— Lily's scared that's why her heart flutters.

— She thinks that maybe she has too much money and kids who don't have so much will feel bad.

— Or the teacher will wonder where she [Lily] got all the money.

— She's careful--she kept the money in a purse pinned to her dress.

— It was good she gave 42 cents to Lena or she [Lily] would have more and get more embarrassed.

— Her heart flutters 'cause she's proud that she can give to the fund. It's her first time.

Such discussions deepen students' understanding of a character's words and actions. Call students' attention to dialogue, setting, and events in books and invite them to talk about the logical conclusions they can draw, always using the text for support.

Talking in small groups or with the entire class allows students to pool ideas and to observe the diversity of thought books worth reading generate. Celebrate students' thinking by recording their ideas on chart paper and hang the chart on a bulletin board for students to reread.

Fourth-grader Laura's Strategy Log entry (Figure 9) shows how much she learned about inferring and drawing conclusions during guided practice and in small group discussions.

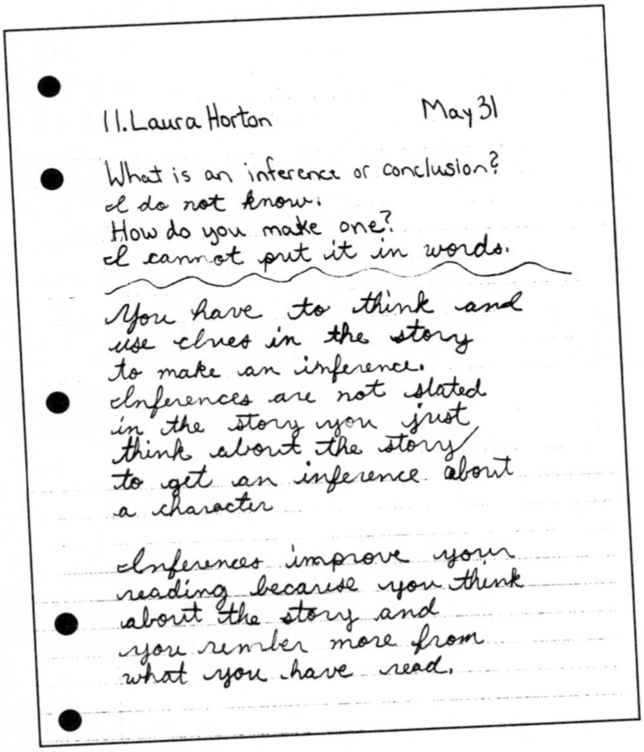

STRATEGY-IN-ACTION: Cause and Effect

Basal reading programs, informal reading inventories, and standardized tests all measure children's critical thinking abilities through cause/effect questions. Given this, it's crucial for us to hone kids' ability to recognize cause and effect. Begin by relating these terms to students' everyday experiences. Explain that an action, such as cleaning your room, can be a cause statement. The effects are the results —things that happen after you clean the room. Third-graders generated this list:

Cause: I cleaned my room.

Effects: I could find things. It's easy to walk there. My mom and dad are happy.

My mom stopped nagging.

I got to go out and play.

Continue using events from the children's lives until they have the concept. Then move to literature. To expand thinking, show students how to write cause statements which, in literature, grow out of problems characters face, issues they deal with, and the actions they take. Problems and issues in history, geography, and science can also be framed in cause statements.

Examples of Cause Statements

📖 *Jack climbs the beanstalk.*

📖 *Goldilocks enters the home of the three bears.*

Figure 9

📖 *Greece is surrounded by water.*

📖 *Weather conditions affect farmers.*

📖 *Earthworms avoid the sun and too much water.*

Work collaboratively on cause statements. On chart paper or the blackboard, record the various effects students offer.

On Their Own

Cause/Effect Lists: Once students show you they can think in terms of cause and effect have them try to sleuth out causes and effects in their own reading. Third-grader Heather writes a cause statement based on *The Littles* by John Peterson (Figure 10). Her list of results demonstrates Heather's ability to select events from the story that result from her cause statement.

Venn Diagram: The Venn diagram, a map consisting of two circles that partially overlap, helps students think about how two items are alike and different. Students fill in similar features in the area that overlaps, and contrasting features in the separate section.

The Venn diagram can be used across the curriculum. You can ask students to compare and contrast characters from two novels or the same character at the beginning and end of a story, or retellings of the same fairy tale or folk tale. With historical texts, students could compare and contrast different wars, governments, values, historical figures, or colonial life in New England and the South. In science, students might compare and contrast different ecosystems, insects, plant and animal cells, or lizards. What you and students study will provide endless possibilities for using the Venn diagram to aid thinking.

Mark, a sixth-grader, used a Venn diagram to show similar and dissimilar features of a green plant and animal cell (Figure 11, page 62). "It was a great way to study for our test because it made everything clear," Mark wrote in his strategy log.

Note-Taking: Students who need to visualize and write in order to remember can take notes using a simple map they design. Such a map, based on information from a textbook, helps students select and logically organize important information. Use maps for class discussions, as study guides for quizzes, and as a writing plan. Here are some mapping tips:

1 Read the passage.

2 Go back and skim the section, scanning headings and words in boldface type.

Heather Rogers November 13

The Littles

The Newcombs arive at the Biggs house.
1. They are happy to be ther.
2. Mr Newcombs said, "Forget about house work."
3. Mrs Newcomb conplans she well have to cook in a strang kitchen.
4. Mr Newcomb said "He is going to loaf."
5 Mr Newcomb said, "It's not my house I'm not going to fix any thing."

Figure 10

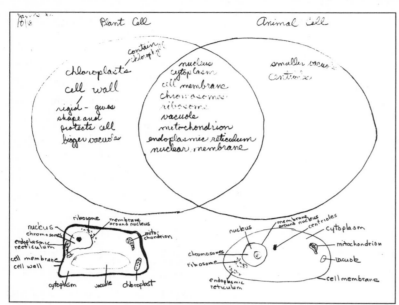

Figure 11

ers film movies on the screen of their mind. Imagining what characters, places, scenes, poems, historical periods, insects, animal, birds, or mathematical computations look like can increase comprehension because learners can visualize only what they understand. Moreover, the more children make pictures and enter the lives of characters, the greater pleasure they may derive from reading.

These mental pictures can be developed with drawings and/or words. Visualization helps students understand how and why characters act and feel, as well as understanding the themes in a book.

The picture can support thinking by supplying evidence that can be explained. Third-graders discussing *The Hallo-Wiener*

3 Decide on the major point of this section. It could be the title of the section. In the center of your paper, place the title inside a circle or above a picture you draw.

4 Think of 4 to 6 categories or headings. Branch lines out from central picture. Write a heading on each line.

5 If you are using the map for writing, each category becomes a separate paragraph.

Fourth-grader Madeline completed her map, of "Tissues and Organs" (Figure 12) after several guided practice sessions. She used the map to study for a quiz. On the back, Madeline wrote everything she remembered after studying her map. Then she compared her written practice with the map. "Now I know what I need to study more," she said. "And I can do it by myself."

Visualize: Creating mental pictures during and after reading is an adventure, as learn-

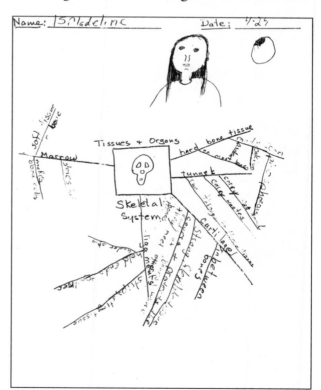

Figure 12

made a list of all the feelings Oscar had throughout the story. See how Rachel connected a visual example of one of Oscar's feelings to words that explain the feeling (Figure 13). Fifth-grader Lauren visualized to select details that show the evil in Lloyd Alexander's *The Book Of Three* (Figure 14).

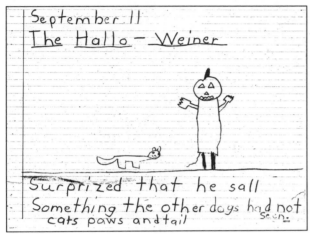

Figure 13

Figure 14

Bookmarks: A self-monitoring strategy, bookmarks encourage readers to interact with a text while reading. Developed by Dorothy Watson and described by Linda K. Crafton in *Whole Language: Getting Started...Moving Forward*, bookmarks can help you observe how students apply reading strategies learned in guided practice to their free-choice reading.

I try not to overuse the technique, however, for constantly writing reactions during reading can detract from enjoyment. Doing it three to four times throughout the school year can supply you and students with sufficient information.

To make bookmarks, fold notebook paper or 8-by-11-inch paper paper in half, lengthwise. Cut into strips and staple two to six sheets together. (The number of sheets depends on the length of the book.)

Have students write their name and the title and author of the book at the top of the first bookmark. As students stop to respond on the bookmark, have them note the page or pages next to their notes.

First I model ways to respond on a bookmark. I explain to students that in addition to applying strategies, they can also note the emotions a passage aroused, connections to other books, or their own lives.

Reluctant readers find it helpful to have written guidelines to help them create bookmarks the first time they try this strategy. On page 64 there are directions you can give students for making bookmarks, suggestions for responding, and a sample bookmark response from a fifth-grader.

Directions for Bookmarks

Say something like:

1 Use your free-choice book.

2 Put your name, and the title and the author of your book at the top of your bookmark.

3 As you respond to your reading, write the page number you stopped on.

4 Here are some ways you can respond:

📖 *Predict what will happen and give support.*

📖 *I reread this part because...*

📖 *Draw a small picture.*

📖 *Ask a question that the story raises.*

📖 *Make a comment on an event or a character.*

📖 *Make a connection to your own life or feelings.*

SAMPLE BOOKMARK RESPONSE

Fifth-grader Robert's response to *The Whipping Boy* by S. Fleischman:

p.1:

What is the hair raising event?
Why is the prince called Brat?
I predict he'll get punished because he played a trick during a big feast.

p. 2:

I wish I had a whipping boy to take my punishments.

Figure 15[1]

Figure 15[2]

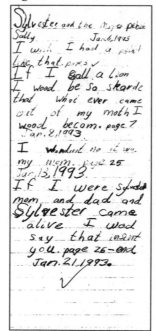

Grade 2 Bookmark   Grade 4 Bookmark

Figure 15[3]

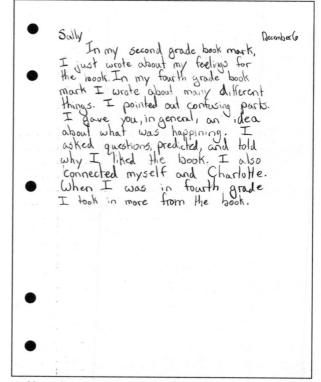

Self-evaluation of both bookmarks

p. 4:

What will happen to the whipping boy?

Bookmarks can also help students set reading goals, for they provide students with a record of their interactions with a text. Sally's bookmarks were completed in grades two and four and self-evaluated in grade five (Figures 15[1], 15[2] and 15[3]).

Some Closing Thoughts

Children who read beyond school assignments, or who choose reading over watching television, are developing a personal reading life. The books they read and the characters in them become important parts of their own lives, influencing the games they play, the dreams they dream, and the thoughts they think. Such deep reading bonds children to books and story.

The strategies discussed in this chapter can help children connect to books by encouraging them to think about, savor, and discuss events, passages, places, and characters.

Lifelong readers turn to books because of the pleasure reading brings to their lives. By offering children strategies that stimulate thinking and wondering, you nurture students' personal reading life.

Vocabulary Building Strategies

When second-grade teacher Carol Chapman asked her class how she could help them become better readers, the overwhelming response was: *Words—what they mean. Words in science and math and history—help us get the hard words so we can read more books and harder ones.*

These youngsters intuitively understood what they needed to move from a beginning level to a proficient level in reading: vocabulary.

Students who read, read, read quite naturally enlarge their vocabulary because they repeatedly meet new words used in different contexts. Repetition helps them figure out the meaning. Each day at school, students are confronted with unfamiliar words, information, and concepts. They are asked to learn and use these words in contexts never before encountered. This is a difficult task.

To build students' vocabularies, students must have a real need for knowing and using the new words when they think, write, and speak.

Because vocabulary knowledge is so crucial to comprehending texts, this chapter will present strategies that develop an understanding of a word's meaning by connecting the word to the concepts students are learning and to what students already know.

Always provide opportunities across the curriculum and throughout the day for students to discuss words; open discussion introduces students to the varied meanings of words.

The dictionary is an invaluable part of word study. Send students to the dictionary after they have talked about new words. Students will be better equipped to comprehend dictionary definitions once they have some background knowledge.

Preparing for Word Studies

Before involving students in word study, identify the concepts in the text that you want students to know. This will help you select only those vocabulary words that are key. When planning a vocabulary study related to our unit on earthquakes, for example, I asked myself questions such as: Is this word necessary for students to comprehend the passage? Is this word crucial to understanding earthquakes? Has the author embedded a clear enough explanation of this term in the passage and/or illustrations?

Choose two to four words. Presenting too many words can overwhelm and frustrate students, causing them to dislike word study. The planning sheet below shows you how I identified key concepts and then had the word study "radiate" from these ideas.

EARTHQUAKE VOCABULARY PLANNING SHEET

Concepts in Chapter:

1 Parts of the earth always move slowly—we don't feel these.

2 It's when the earth moves quickly that we have an earthquake.

3 Shifts in the earth cause waves that spread out and can be measured on a scale called the Richter Scale.

4 Most earthquakes happen in the earth's crust.

New Words to Teach Before Class Reads Chapter:

1 seismic waves

2 seismometer

3 fault—do in double entry journal

4 Crust, mantle, outer core, inner core—build clay model and slice

Familiar Ideas and Words to Build On:

1 seismic waves—waves in the ocean and how you feel them on a boat

2 seismometer—devices that measures things—scales, lie detector, electric cardiogram

3 fault—crack in an eggshell, in wood, in a plate

Once you identify the concepts and key words, you will need to discover what students know about these concepts. The three strategies that follow invite students, prior to reading, to think deeply about meaning and how a word functions in our language.

STRATEGY-IN-ACTION: Vocabulary Connections

Set aside 15 to 20 minutes at least twice each week to introduce one word. Record the process on large chart paper and hang the charts on a wall so students can reread them throughout the study.

The steps below illustrate how I linked what students already knew about *fault* to its meaning in the chapter on earthquakes:

1 Think of a synonym students might have for the new word. I use *crack* as a synonym for *fault* and ask students, "What happens when you crack something?" After exchanging anecdotes, I introduce the word *fault*.

2 On chart paper, I print what students know about *crack*, then write the word *fault* on the next line.

3 Next, students skim the chapter, pausing to read with care those sections that discuss *fault*.

4 Students talk in groups sharing what they understand about the new word and find situations where they might use *fault*. I write these on the chart under the heading "Situations."

5 Invite groups to find synonyms, or words with similar meanings, and record these on the chart under "Other Ways of Saying *fault*."

6 On the chart, model several ways the words work in sentences.

7 On another day, after students reread the chapter, they create sentences that I print on the chart.

8 Ask students to see what information the dictionary offers. Now they are ready to expand their knowledge of this new word.

9 Display the chart and use the word frequently.

Chart for the Word *Fault*

fault
What Students Already Know

- *A crack can ruin a dish or glass.*
- Crack *means to break.*
- *Crack wood or a watermelon and you break it in pieces.*
- *Cracking something, like a log, can make 2 parts.*

Other Ways of Saying *Fault*

break

crack

imperfection

fracture

Situations

- *when layers of rock under the earth break*
- *a break in rock that makes 2 separate sections*
- *a break in rock under the sea*
- *sections of the earth push against each other and meet*

Some Students' Sentences

1 A fault in layers of rock makes the rock bend.

2 The San Andreas Fault is near the coast of California.

3 The fault in those underwater mountains caused an earthquake.

STRATEGY-IN-ACTION:
Guess and Adjust

First tell students the topic or theme, so they have some data to plug into a guess. Ask students to guess the meaning of two to three new words (this can arouse their curiosity about key words prior to reading). Record their ideas on chart paper. First work with the entire class, so that students reluctant to guess can observe that, at this point, guesses are way off-target.

After students read a selection, have them reread the passage that contains the word, study the pictures, and then adjust their guesses. The most important part of this strategy is the time spent on sharing guesses and adjustments. Such talk drives students back to the text, taps into their prior knowledge, and offers all members an opportunity to think deeply about words and concepts.

Work collaboratively and model the process several times before inviting students to work alone. Invite groups to share their guesses and adjustments and add additional meanings in their journals. A great deal of information surfaces as groups exchange ideas.

Sample Group Discussion

The transcription below is of third graders discussing *contribute* after they completed guessing and adjusting.

B: I learned it means you give money like Lily wanted to give.

J: It can mean to give to others--but it is not just money.

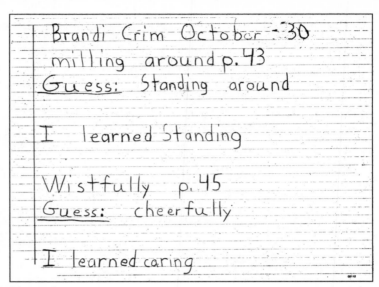

Figure 1

G: You can give help like when we went to the soup kitchen.

B: But in this book it means money for the Pedestal Fund. Or at Christmas when you give to the Salvation Army.

G: Or at church when they pass the silver plates.

J: It's what we're doing now--we're contributing our ideas.

Discussion enabled these third-graders to move beyond the meaning in their book and explore other definitions and uses of *contribute*.

Students can guess, read, and adjust in small groups, or pairs, then alone. Third-grader Brandi practices "guess and adjust" in her strategy log before reading chapter 6 of *Lily and Miss Liberty* (Figure 1). Fifth-grader Jaime uses this strategy prior to studying the solar system (Figure 2).

STRATEGY-IN-ACTION:
Word Association Webs

Constructing word association webs, also

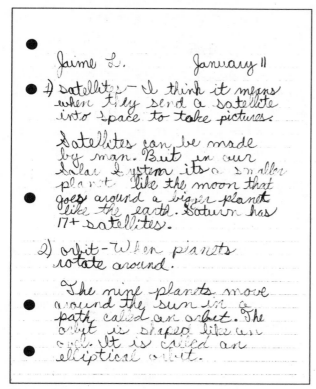

Figure 2

good example of how sixth-graders, prior to a theme study on prejudice, became aware of related words such as *stereotype*, *xenophobia*, and *intolerant*.

Word webs entice students to think of words related to a topic and then organize these words under meaningful headings. You might work as a class, dividing students into small groups, and follow these steps:

1 On large chart paper, the teacher writes the word, topic, or concept.

2 Students write their name and date on a clean journal page.

3 Groups discuss the topic or theme for five to ten minutes, giving examples from their own experiences.

4 Students work silently for five to eight minutes and list in their journals all the ideas recalled from discussion.

5 Students share ideas, one at a time; the teacher records these on a chart.

6 Groups study the chart and think of categories for the ideas.

7 The teacher collects suggestions for categories, and the class decides which ones to use.

called semantic mapping, is a vocabulary-building strategy developed by Johnson and Pearson in 1984. Used before reading, the strategy helps students reclaim what they already know about a word or concept. The concept map on prejudice (Figure 3) is a

8 The teacher prepares a web, with the word in the middle and categories that branch out from the word.

9 Students place words under categories. Some words will fit under more than one category. Ask students to discuss why this is appropriate.

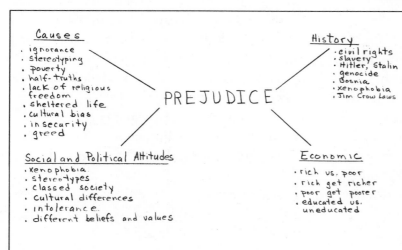

Figure 3

Continue to work collaboratively with younger students, and display their webs in a prominent place. Once older students understand how to construct a "word association web," have them complete the entire process in small groups or with partners.

After reading and discussing new material, students return to the web to adjust ideas and add new words and phrases. Revisiting the prereading web allows students to integrate new knowledge with what they already knew.

Invite Students to Identify New Words

It's helpful for students to have simple strategies to identify words they don't understand before and during reading. Your students will be more willing to invest the time it takes to learn new words if they do the selecting. Help students keep track of unfamiliar words by having them write these words on a sticky note, or index card or on a journal page. The strategies that follow invite students to pinpoint unfamiliar words.

STRATEGY-IN-ACTION: Browse and Find

This strategy prepares students for difficult words they will meet prior to reading. Before beginning a theme, author, or research study or a unit in a textbook, invite students to identify unfamiliar words by browsing through books and magazines or having them skim the textbook chapter. Divide students into pairs or small groups, so they can talk about the words and topic and exchange ideas. Words that several students have identified can be discussed with the whole class.

STRATEGY-IN-ACTION: Vocabulary Wall

Tape a large piece of chart or construction paper on a wall that children can easily reach. Place several marker pens in a box next to the wall chart. Have children write unfamiliar words on the chart after they have completed a sustained silent reading period. Words can also come from reading completed at home.

For whole-class instruction, I select words that appear on the chart several times. Small groups and pairs can select words to discuss and study. Many students will use the words on the vocabulary wall as a spelling resource for writing new words correctly.

Some Vocabulary Building Strategies for During and After Reading

The strategies in this section offer students opportunities to think about words during and after reading. Over time, new words become part of students' spoken and written vocabulary. To enlarge vocabulary, students continuously refine meanings through reading and discussion and also observe how these words function in different written and spoken contexts. Learners need to take risks and try out new words.

Second-grader Jenny, concerned about a member of her group, said to her teacher, "Miss Hall, Miss Hall, Donald needs your help. He's sick. He's…he's…constipated." The word caught the children's attention. All eyes were on Jenny. No one laughed. Instead, Donald pointed to his red, swollen nose and said, "I'm congested." Then he put his head on his desk. This story not only illustrates Jenny's caring attitude, but it also shows her willingness to try a new word. Her classmates, encouraged to take risks in order to learn, chose to support Jenny, not put her down. That day, Jenny gained a deeper understanding of two words which had sounded the same to her. Donald's bad cold helped her construct a clearer concept of "congestion," but certainly, not all the meanings that word conveys.

At best, when students first meet new words, they gain an awareness of the word's meaning and how it connects to concepts they already know. Repeatedly using the word can help children move from awareness to solidly incorporating the word into their vocabulary.

STRATEGY-IN-ACTION: Read On, Then Reread

When students meet an unfamiliar word that confuses them, you can offer the strategy Read On, then Reread. Tell students that adults meet unfamiliar words and need strategies to help them unravel meaning. In a minilesson, model what you do when you come to a word you don't know.

Things You Can Do When You Come To a Word You Don't Understand

1 Skip the confusing word and read to the end of the sentence, looking for clues. Very often, the author supplies the meaning of a difficult word right in the sentence.

2 Continue reading to find a clue or reread two to three sentences that came before the confusing part.

3 Study the illustrations or diagrams on that page.

4 Think about what you already know about the topic.

5 Reread the difficult section, sometimes several times, in order to comprehend the word.

6 Jot down the word on a sticky note or index card or in your journal, if you're still unsure of its meaning.

7 Print word on the "Word Wall" or bring it before your group for discussion.

Quite often, students know what a word means, but they can not pronounce the word. Telling students to "sound out" the word is too general a direction. When I ask students what "sounding out" means, most repeat the phrase and tell me, "you just try to sound it out." Such responses tell me that students don't have specific strategies. Therefore, it's important repeatedly to demonstrate many ways to solve this reading problem. Have students read in pairs when they are using a difficult text so partners can support one another.

Things You Can Do When You Can't Pronounce a Word

1 Look at the beginning and ending letters.

2 Look for small, familiar words or patterns within the word.

3 Look for prefixes and suffixes you can pronounce.

4 Look for a familiar base or root word.

5 Separate the word into segments and say each part.

6 Look for compound words and see if you can say one word.

7 Go back and reread the sentence, trying to pronounce the word.

8 If you still can't pronounce the word, substitute a word that makes sense and continue reading. Use picture and meaning clues from the text to make an "educated guess."

9 Jot down the word on a sticky note or in your journal.

10 Place the word on the "Word Wall" and ask your reading buddy or group to discuss the word.

STRATEGY-IN-ACTION: Visualizing Words

Creating mental pictures evoked by words during reading or illustrating a word after reading a selection can deepen understanding. It is only possible to draw the meaning of a word that is clearly understood.

Fourth-graders, reading a section of *African Journey*, drew pictures to understand the difference between *dotted* and *skirted*. Sally's picture and written explanation demonstrate her knowledge of these words. In her strategy log, Sally explains that her picture definitions are easier to recall than her writing definitions (Figures 4, 5).

When Vocabulary Strategies Don't Work

 ometimes students will not have success with a strategy. It's likely that these students don't have enough prior knowledge or experience. This means you will have to rethink your demonstrations and find a way to connect students to the concept.

When a strategy doesn't work, we often blame ourselves. This was the case with Heather, a fifth-grade teacher who is a member of my reading strategy networking group. Heather opened one of our meetings

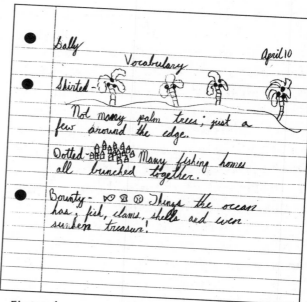

Figure 4

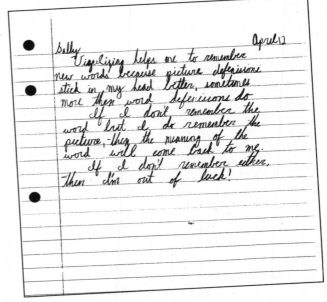

Figure 5

by describing her frustrating experience using the "Vocabulary Connections" strategy with fifth-graders reading at a primer level. "I was trying to get them to understand *habitat* by first asking them to think about homes and places where people and animals live. They couldn't get beyond house numbers and street names. I'm sure I did something wrong."

The group helped Heather stop blaming herself and entertain the possibility that the students did not have enough prior knowledge about home and environment. That morning, Heather left armed with two suggestions: 1) Take students outside and talk about bird, insect, and plant habitats; 2) Bring in pictures of animals and people living in different habitats and have students discuss these. At the next meeting Heather couldn't wait to tell her colleagues how well the suggestions had worked!

Lack of prior knowledge can stump learners, making it difficult to read and think about new concepts. Below are some experiences you can give students to enlarge their prior knowledge:

- *Select books and magazine articles to read aloud.*

- *Show a video.*

- *Look at and discuss photographs and illustrations.*

- *Take a field trip.*

- *Bring in materials for students to touch and talk about.*

- *Invite experts to your classroom.*

- *Use the school grounds.*

You can also provide a system of support for students who struggle with vocabulary.

Organize class reading buddies or small reading teams that change throughout the year. Make sure each team includes a child who can provide support. Encourage students to seek help from a buddy or a team member when they confront an unfamiliar word or confusing passage.

On Their Own

We need words to read, to write, to think, and to speak. As you incorporate new words into your discussions and minilessons, ask students to engage in some of these suggested vocabulary building activities:

- *Make an illustrated dictionary or word book (see sample, Figures 6¹–6¹², on page 76)*

- *Build a list of synonyms and/or antonyms.*

- *Use the word in writing and speaking.*

- *Explain the word to a partner.*

- *Use the dictionary to verify meanings.*

- *Find out the history, or etymology, of a word.*

Some Closing Thoughts

Words are the very basic and useful tools of readers, writers, thinkers, and talkers. The words we own determine our ability to think, understand, write, formulate, and communicate ideas. Therefore, vocabulary building is central to all reading development, because learning new words and concepts enables children to deal with more difficult and complex texts. Children with limited vocabularies experience great diffi-

Jennifer's word Book

tornado

hort

damage turn

Figure 6¹

tornado

Figure 6²

tornados are pawerful they can do alot of damage. it can hert peopl vary bad. It can kill peopl it can kill eny thing. it starts by Hot and wate and cold.

Figure 6³

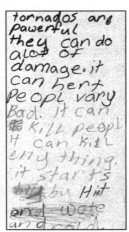

damage

Figure 6⁴

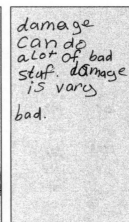

damage can do alot of bad stuf. damage is vary bad.

Figure 6⁵

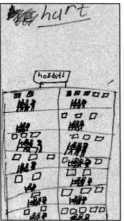

hurt

hosbitl

Figure 6⁶

hurt

Tornato can hart alot of Peopl. and you wod have to go to the hosbil.

Figure 6⁷

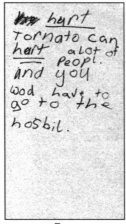

turn

Figure 6⁸

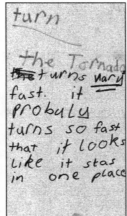

turn

the Tornado turns vary fast. it probuly turns so fast that it looks like it stas in one place

Figure 6⁹

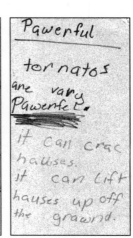

Pawerful

tornatos are vary Pawerfel.

It can crac hauses. It can lift hauses up off the graund.

Figure 6¹⁰

Figures 6 ¹–6 ¹². Word book on the word "powerful" by Jennifer, Grade 2.

Pawerful

damage

THE ENE

turn   torna

hurt

Figure 6¹¹

Powerful

Figure 6¹²

culty comprehending texts and communicating with others.

New words can become part of children's vocabularies when instruction helps children link what they already know to the new and unfamiliar concepts. Once a connection has been made, children can work on refining their initial awareness of the word's meaning, slowly increase their understanding, and eventually remember and use the word in reading, speech, and writing.

Debriefings and Conferences

During debriefings and conferences, children exchange experiences with and understandings of reading strategies in order to spotlight the ways a particular strategy supported reading comprehension. At these meetings teachers encourage students to reflect on and self-monitor the reading strategies they use on their own and during guided practice. Both activities foster self-evaluation and the setting of reasonable goals.

Debriefing in a Fourth Grade Class

Fourth-graders talk about their recent experiences with visualizing the meaning of new words. We

draft questions to guide conversations: How did making mental pictures help? What did I learn about the word? What did I learn about how much I understood? How did this strategy help my reading?

First, groups exchange thoughts and offer examples from strategy logs. Then they share their reactions, which I record on chart paper. Sally suggests I set up three categories: BEFORE, DURING, and AFTER, so we can "see on the chart how it worked all the ways we did it." The chart on page 78 summarizes the reflective talk of these fourth-graders.

These students were debriefing, exchanging all the information they had learned about a vocabulary strategy. Unlike a military debriefing, whose purpose is to collect information to determine what to make

BEFORE	DURING	AFTER
Helped us begin to think about words.	Had to reread to get the meaning.	The picture made me remember meaning better.
If I couldn't make a picture I got mad—I didn't understand it.	Had to understand more than the word to make pictures.	Once I could see the word, I could use in a sentence.
I looked for the word in the book to see if it matched my picture.	Began to make pictures of the places and characters.	I pictured the letters of the word, too.
First I thought this was stupid.	Making pictures got me into the book.	The pictures helped keep it in my head.

Fourth Grade debriefing chart on "Visualizing"

public and what to keep secret, a reading strategy debriefing strives to make all feelings and reactions public.

Writing their observations on the chart creates a permanent record students can return to again and again; they can also revise their first reactions. The process encourages me to consider what worked and what could be improved; I always share my thoughts with students. For example, after reviewing the chart, I pointed out how pleased I was that they were rereading and making pictures of characters and settings as well as of some words. Several students felt frustrated because they couldn't draw a word prior to reading. "Doing it that way didn't help, it just made us mad," they told me.

My intention was to have them think about why they couldn't illustrate a word prior to reading, but could draw a picture after reading. No doubt, the frustration wasn't productive. The students' honesty helped me evaluate and rethink my plans.

When to Debrief

"When should we debrief?" and "How often should we debrief?" are two questions I wrestle with all the time. Unfortunately, there is no prescribed schedule. Most of the time, students and I debrief after one or several collaborative practices. My one rule of thumb is to make sure I've held at least two debriefings before inviting students to work independently or in pairs. Making students' reactions public encourages reflection, enlarges students' knowledge of how a strategy works, pinpoints misconceptions and/or confusing steps, and sends the powerful message that it is important work.

Creating Successful Debriefings

Debriefing is a learned process, and your job is to model how it works with the entire class before moving to small group discussions.

Help students understand that thinking about all reactions, not judging a student's ideas, will increase their knowledge about how a strategy works.

Second-grade teacher Carol Chapman leads a whole class debriefing after she has had several whole or small group lessons on predicting and offering support. Students discussed these questions: *How does predicting help my reading? How do I feel about finding evidence from the story? What happens to my predictions as I read more of the story?*

Second-Graders' Debriefing on Making Predictions

— Made me think more about the story. When something I predicted didn't happen, I had to think more.

— I could make predictions when I try to write my own story.

— I liked confirming better than adjusting. Getting reasons is hard.

— Finding reasons from the story made me remember more.

— At the beginning it was more like guessing. At the end we could figure out the story.

— It kept me interested—I wanted to see if I had to make adjustments.

— Face it, it's fun!

These thoughts demonstrate a high level of involvement in and enthusiasm for predicting. Making adjustments was difficult for some students, even though Carol reread the story several times. The debriefing process identified those students who struggled with finding evidence from the text to support predictions. Carol now had a topic to discuss at a reading conference with a student. She was also able to identify students who might benefit from additional, teacher-led practice before working with a partner or alone.

After students understand a strategy, Carol invites them to teach and practice it with their parents. Then each child debriefs mom, dad, or an adult at home on the reading strategy and brings the results to their group and/or the class.

When parents experience reading strategies by having their children guide them, parents gain an appreciation of the process and the teacher's purposes. Second-grader Jonathan told the class, "My mom said that predicting and going back to fix them [predictions] really made her think more. She liked doing it with me and asked if we could do it again."

Sometimes, the connections we hope students will make during a debriefing surface in other classes. Days later, during a discussion of weather, Clarke, a second grader in Carol Chapman's class, observed, "Weathermen take information and make predictions about what it will be like tomorrow—it's like what we do reading a book."

Developing Questions for Debriefing Conversations

T he purpose of developing questions for debriefing sessions is to identify how a strategy worked and supported recall and comprehension. Ask students to raise questions they have about a strategy after minilessons and before debriefings; add those you feel will be helpful.

Sample Open-ended Debriefing Questions

📖 *Did you adapt or change the strategy? How and Why?*

📖 *Did the strategy help you remember details?*

📖 *How do you feel about the strategy?*

📖 *How did the strategy help your reading?*

Self-Evaluation

I n addition to debriefing sessions, students can reflect on how they integrate strategies into their reading by responding to the checklist on page 81. The list can be shortened to reflect the strategies students have practiced. To make the list meaningful, ask students to discuss it with a partner, small group, or at a teacher-student reading conference. Students can write a self-evaluative paragraph after discussion, in Figures 1[1] and 1[2], on this page, Sally reacts to and evaluates her own notes on *Banshee*.

Scheduled Conferences

O ne-on-one conferences allow you to observe how children use, adapt, and modify reading strategies. You'll want to meet with reluctant and struggling readers more frequently so you can provide supportive suggestions and additional practice. My goal is to have at least one twenty-minute reading conference with each student every marking period. Set a positive tone by opening the conference with the progress and growth you've observed. Topics for reading strategy con-

Figure 1[1]

Figure 1[2]

ferences can come from the following:

📖 *Reading strategy interviews*

📖 *Students' responses to the seven questions about reading*

Continued on page 82

A READING STRATEGY CHECKLIST

Name _____ Date _____

Directions: Check those statements that reflect the strategies you use.

Strategies I Use Before Reading

_____ I think about the cover, title, and topic.

_____ I read the back cover and the print on the inside of the jacket.

_____ I ask questions.

_____ I predict.

_____ I skim the pictures, charts, and graphs.

_____ I read headings and words in bold-faced type.

_____ I think about what I know about the topic.

Strategies I Use While Reading

_____ I stop and check to see if I understand what I'm reading.

_____ I make mental pictures.

_____ I identify confusing parts.

_____ I identify unfamiliar words.

_____ I reread to understand confusing parts and unfamiliar words.

_____ I record an unfamiliar word that I can't figure out.

_____ I use pictures, graphs, and charts to help me understand confusing parts.

_____ I stop and retell to check what I remember.

_____ I reread to remember more details.

_____ I read the captions under and above photographs, charts, graphs, etc.

_____ I predict and adjust as I read.

_____ I raise questions and read for answers.

Strategies I Use After Reading

_____ I think about why I liked it.

_____ I retell.

_____ I speak, draw, and/or write reactions.

_____ I reread favorite parts.

_____ I reread to find details.

_____ I picture characters and places and ideas.

_____ I predict what might happen to a character if the story continued.

- 📖 *Teacher observations*
- 📖 *Reactions to minilessons*
- 📖 *Students' strategy logs*
- 📖 *Students' reading logs*
- 📖 *Student requests*
- 📖 *Debriefing sessions*
- 📖 *Self-evaluation check list*
- 📖 *Oral and written retellings*
- 📖 *Students' Bookmarks and teachers' reactions*

Here are some guidelines that have made conferences productive for my class:

- 📖 *Discover what students want to discuss by asking them to bring items, topics, and questions to the conference.*

- 📖 *If you plan the conference, let students know the topic in advance, so they can come prepared. Always reserve some time for students to tell you their needs during a preplanned conference.*

- 📖 *Be a good listener. Let students do the talking. Wait for students to respond to a query, even though it feels like a long, long time.*

- 📖 *Nudge students to try a strategy by practicing the strategy during the conference and then talking about the benefits.*

- 📖 *During the last five minutes of the conference, invite students to tell you the highlights of the conference and set a goal. Talk about the new goal during mini-conferences.*

It's mid-December and Matt, a second grader, requests a conference after he has completed his written retelling of *The Story of Ferdinand* by Munro Leaf. Before Matt opens his strategy log to read, he tells me, "It took me lots of days to write this."

I listen carefully as Matt reads aloud his retelling. When Matt has finished, I tell him how much I enjoyed his retelling, especially the rich details and the sequencing of the plot. Then I wait for Matt's reaction to my comments. He tells me that he liked working on this, but it was hard work and took a lot of concentration. "I couldn't do it for every book," he explains. I ask Matt why he feels that way. "Well," he replies, pausing to think, "I would lose reading time. I could reread what I don't remember and do it in my head."

As Matt talks, I take notes. He summarizes, on paper, the high points of the conference and sets a goal (Figure 2). Such records are important because it is impossi-

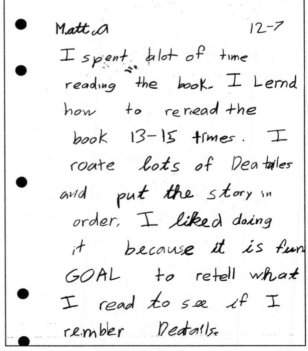

Matt A   12-7
I spent a lot of time reading the book. I Lernd how to reread the book 13-15 times. I roate lots of Deatales and put the story in order. I liked doing it because it is fun GOAL to retell what I read to see if I rember Deatails.

Figure 2

ble to remember the details of each conference. Moreover, written notes help you and students monitor progress and set goals, and can also be used at conferences with parents and administrators.

I request a retelling conference with Ginna, another second-grader, after she expresses doubts about her retelling. (While circulating around the room, I had asked Ginna what she thought of her retelling, and she had responded by saying "I don't know," several times.) Through a conference, I want Ginna to see what a fine job she had done. Here is the transcription of my conference with Ginna (Figure 3, at right).

R: Looks like you've written four pages here.

G: Well, we had to write lots of things and keep them in order.

R: Read your retelling to me. [Ginna reads.] How do you feel about your retelling?

G: [Giggles] I still don't know.

R: How could you tell?

G: Ask if I did the things. I wrote four pages. It's a lot if you can fill up so many pages. I had lots of the story. [Ginna rereads silently.] Yes--I think it's in order. I like it.

R: I agree. You had all of the important parts of the story in the order each happened. I like the specific details like how Ferdinand felt and what the bull ring looked like.

G: I read the book three times myself before I started to retell.

R: Why three times?

G: So I could know what to say alone. Our

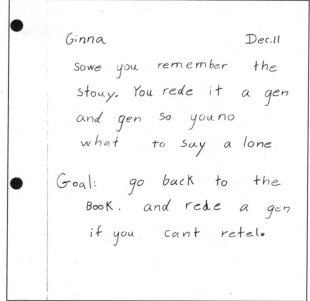

Figure 3   *Ginna's summary and goal after our conference on retelling.*

group told it together and hearing helped me remember too.

R: How did you feel when you wrote the retelling?

G: I had to read it two more times and then it was easy. I got stuck near the end.

R: What did you do?

G: I looked at the book!

Making the Rounds

Circulating among students during reading times lets you follow-up on a student's goal, provide support with independent application of a strategy, and respond to students' questions. Clipboard in hand, you can note observations and snippets of conversations as you circulate around the classroom.

You will also want to model how important reading is to you during these times. I announce to students that I will read during the first fifteen minutes of reading-writing workshop or Sustained Silent Reading, then make the rounds. I always share the book I am reading with the class and briefly talk about my reactions.

Making the rounds keeps me in close touch with students' progress and needs. It's a strategy that encourages teacher observation of and interactions with students, helping me quickly spot problems.

Some Closing Thoughts

When students debrief after they have practiced a strategy, I listen carefully. Since debriefings occur more frequently than formal conferences, this is an ideal time to learn how the children have integrated a strategy into the reading process.

It can be a challenge to schedule formal conferences even three to four times a year. It's much easier to schedule more frequent debriefings, making the rounds, and having students write self-evaluations, which are quite manageable and packed with valuable insights into your students' process and progress.

Putting It All Together

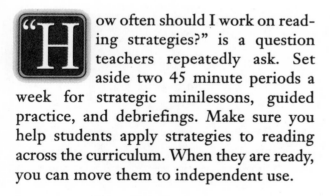

"How often should I work on reading strategies?" is a question teachers repeatedly ask. Set aside two 45 minute periods a week for strategic minilessons, guided practice, and debriefings. Make sure you help students apply strategies to reading across the curriculum. When they are ready, you can move them to independent use.

Which Strategies Do I Teach?

As stated in Chapter One, I feel it's nearly impossible to develop hard and fast guidelines for teaching specific strategies at each grade level. However, by collaborating with other teachers in your school, you can develop guidelines to suit your students, like the ones on page 86,

which can be reviewed and revised yearly. Guidelines are merely suggestions, and some teachers will go beyond these while others will not get to every suggested strategy. The issue is not how much you cover, but communicating what students have learned so adjustments can be made by next year's teacher.

The plan on the following page originally appeared in Chapter One. It is reviewed here.

Of course, you will emphasize some strategies more than others. Trust your instincts and your expertise. Some students will practice one particular strategy longer than others. You will often work on more than one strategy. For example, while you're practicing making predictions with fiction, students will be learning questioning and/or note-taking techniques in science and social

GRADE 2	GRADE 3	GRADE 4
Predict	Predict	Predict
Retell	Retell	Question
Question	Question	Reread
Reread	Reread	Read-Pause-Retell
Vocabulary: Guessing	Vocab. Webs	All Vocab. strategies
Browse	Vocab. Discussion	Skim
K-W-H-L	Charts	Brainstorm
Vocab. Connections	Vocab. Connections	Visualize
Visualize	K-W-H-L	Fast Write
Brainstorm	Visualize	Bookmarks
Bookmarks	Bookmarks	Reading Rate
Skim	Read-Pause-Retell	K-W-H-L
Reading Rate	Reading Rate	Cause/Effect
Cause/Effect	Cause/Effect	Context Clues
Context Clues	Context Clues	Confusing parts
Identify confusing parts	Confusing parts	Self-correct
Self-correct	Self-correct	Venn Diagram
Book Selection	Venn Diagram	Book Selection
	Book Selection	

GRADE 5	GRADE 6
Summarize	Summarize
Fast Write	Skim
All of grade 4	Note-taking
Review all strategies when necessary.	Review all strategies when necessary.

studies. You'll discuss reading rate, skimming, visualizing, and rereading in several subjects. The list is simply a reference guide. Each year it will change because each year you and the students you teach will be different. And each year you and students will revisit strategies practiced in the previous grade. Revisiting allows students to gain deeper insights into strategies and to reconstruct what they already know by integrating the new experiences they continue to have.

Evaluation of Students' Progress

Collecting evidence of how students apply reading strategies to new material as well as data from conferences and strategy logs can supply you with concrete examples of growth. The chart that follows lists a variety of applications you can collect.

Documenting Assessments

In addition to taking notes, it's helpful to have a checklist of assessment guidelines. Such forms can be used during a student-teacher conference; they help teacher's quickly organize their thoughts. Together, students and teachers can select items to address and add an item not included on the list.

Knowing how to design a checklist will enable you and colleagues to create assessment tools for many strategies. Here is what I do:

📖 *Heading: name the strategy.*

📖 *Provide space for student's name*

BEFORE READING	WHILE READING	AFTER READING
Brainstorming	Predict & Support	Predict & Support
Fast write	Poses questions	Prediction Book Report
Book selection	Question Guide	Venn Diagram
Participates in whole class or small group activity	Identifies confusing vocabulary	Vocabulary Web
	Reacts in a journal	Cause/Effect Chart
	Rereads	Retelling
		Journal responses
		Summaries
		Discussions
		Question Guide
		Speech
		Reader's Theater Script
		Writes discussion questions

and date and, if applicable, the title and author of book used.

📖 *Create a rating key such as: Rarely, Sometimes, Most of the Time, Not Applicable.*

📖 *List the elements of the strategy.*

📖 *Provide space to list strengths—what worked well.*

📖 *Provide space to list needs*

📖 *Provide space for student to write reactions to the assessment and, if appropriate, set a goal that emerges from the conference.*

I've included a sample assessment checklist for a written retelling completed by third-grader Gregory (Figure 1[1], at right, and Figure 1[2], page 89). A written prediction/support piece by sixth-grader Maria is on page 89 (Figures 2[1] and 2[2]). Assessing and monitoring students' independent use of strategies during conferences lets you quickly identify those, like Maria, who require additional support and monitoring.

Pinpointing Students Who Make Little Progress

E ach year you will have one or more students who arrive as weak readers and seem to make little progress. I find it extremely helpful to use the checklist Reading Difficulty Indicators (sample on pages 90 and 91) to detect students who need help. The list forces me to reflect carefully on a student's work, to gather specific evidence, and to isolate areas that need help. The more specific data you have, the better equipped you'll be to design a teaching plan that might consist of one-on-one tutoring,

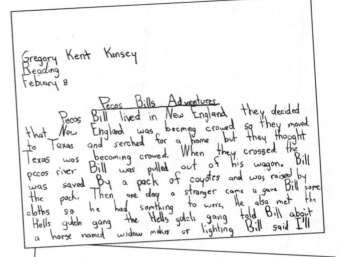

Figure 1[1]   *Gregory's written retelling.*

additional conferences to support and monitor progress, or an after school reading buddy.

It's a good idea to invite other teachers who work with a student to complete the checklist. Then, confer with a team of teachers to brainstorm interventions that will encourage growth and progress in reading.

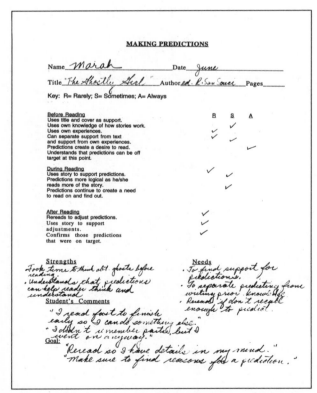

RETELLING

Name _Gregory Kinsey_   Date _Feb. 8_

Title _Pecos Bill_   Author _Steven Kellogg_   Pages _entire book_

Key: R= Rarely; S= Sometimes; A= Always

                         R   S   A

Setting
Tells where and when the story takes place.
Characters and Problems
Names main character and problems he/she faced.
Names other characters and shows how these
connect to main character.
Plot
Tells "X" number of events.
Sequences the events.
Includes rich details.
Includes beginning/middle/end of story.
Demonstrates an understanding of concepts
and information.
Solution
Shows how problems were solved.
Personal Connections
Offers feelings and reactions.
Makes connections between characters.
and events in own life.
Presentation
Speaks fluently.
Uses vocabulary from text. _yes_

written retelling
read it to one
fluently, and with
great expression

Strengths
· rich details - shows super effort
· well sequenced
· showed how each adventure resolves
· included dialogue
· enthusiasm and pleasure show

Needs
· some personal reactions to
  the story and characters
· discuss illustrations
  and genre during our
  talk about the story

Student's Comments
"I read the story 5 times and worked hard."
"I can talk about other ideas because I know the story
  like what kind of person Pecos Bill was."
"I can use retelling to myself to tell what I remember."

Goal: "To think about how I feel about a story."

Figure 1²   *Retelling Checklist*

MAKING PREDICTIONS

Name _Marah_   Date _June_

Title _"The Ghostly Girl"_   Author _ed. R. San Souci_   Pages ___

Key: R= Rarely; S= Sometimes; A= Always

                         R   S   A

Before Reading
Uses title and cover as support.
Uses own knowledge of how stories work.
Uses own experiences.
Can separate support from text
and support from own experiences.
Predictions create a desire to read.
Understands that predictions can be off
target at this point.

During Reading
Uses story to support predictions.
Predictions more logical as he/she
reads more of the story.
Predictions continue to create a need
to read on and find out.

After Reading
Rereads to adjust predictions.
Uses story to support
adjustments.
Confirms those predictions
that were on target.

Strengths
Took time to think abt. ghosts before
reading.
· Understands that predictions
  can help reader think and
  understand.

Needs
· To find support for
  predictions.
· To separate predicting from
  writing prior knowledge.
· Reread if don't recall
  enough to predict.

Student's Comments
"I read fast to finish
 early so I can do something else."
"I didn't remember parts, but I
 went on anyway."

Goal: "Reread so I have details in my mind."
"Make sure to find reasons for a prediction."

Figure 2¹   *Maria's Written Prediction/*
Support Piece

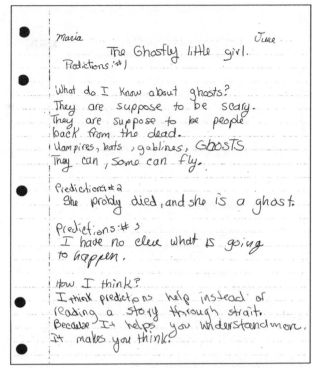

Maria   _June_

      The Ghostly little girl.

Predictions #1

What do I know about ghosts?
They are suppose to be scary.
They are suppose to be people
back from the dead.
Vampires, bats, goblines, Ghosts
They can, some can fly.

Predictions #2
She probly died, and she is a ghost.

Predictions #3
I have no clue what is going
to happen.

How I think?
I think predictions help instead of
reading a story through strait.
Because It helps you understand more.
It makes you think?

Figure 2²   *Maria's Prediction Checklist*

Organizing Your Paper Work

On page 92 is a list of records you and students keep for a strategic reading program. Pulling these records together will streamline the program so that recordkeeping takes minimal time.

Don't try to do everything the first year. The suggested time line below will help you set reasonable goals.

Year One: Introduce Strategy Logs; conduct strategy interviews; collaborate with colleagues to plan minilessons; save minilesson charts for rereading; collect samples of students' independent applications.

Year Two: Keep a Planning Journal; start a folder of stories for guided practice; analyze students' responses to the seven ques-

READING DIFFICULTY INDICATORS: A Checklist

Name _____

Key: R= Rarely; S= Sometimes; M= Most of the Time

KNOWLEDGE OF HOW PRINT WORKS:	R	S	M
Matches letters to sounds			
Segments words			
Attends to medial sounds			
Random guesses			
Skips lines and/or words			
Word-to-word reading			
Identifies randomly written alphabet letters			
Uses left-to-right directionality with print			
Points to beginning or end of page			
Shows knowledge of narrative structure and elements			

COMPREHENSION OF TEXT:			
Aware of decoding errors and their relationship to meaning			
Stops/pauses at punctuation			
Detailed retellings			
Recalls story details sequentially			
Recalls factual information			
Uses the following reading strategies:			
predict/confirm or adjust			
question			
visualize			
reread			
uses prior knowledge			

Continued...

READING DIFFICULTY INDICATORS: A Check List

Page 2

Key: R= Rarely; S= Sometimes; M= Most of the Time

	R	S	M
uses 4 cueing systems to solve problems: semantic, contextual, syntactic, graphophonic			
Has a solid grade-level sight vocabulary			
Has rich experiences and prior knowledge to comprehend texts			
Has many literacy experiences			
Understands cause/effect, compare/contrast, and infers meaning from characters' actions, words			
Substitutes words that do not connect to meaning of passage			
Sub-vocalizes text when reading silently			

READING ATTITUDES:

	R	S	M
Sees self as a reader			
Sees purpose of reading			
Sees reading as using past knowledge to create new understandings			
Is self-monitoring			
Has an independent reading life			
Relates text to own experiences			

Notes: _____

_____

_____

_____

_____

STUDENTS	TEACHERS
Strategy Log	Planning Journal
Independent Applications	Reading Interviews
	Notes on Students' Responses to the Seven Questions
	Reading Conference Notes
	Strategy Assessment Checklists
	Story File For Guided Practice
	Samples of students' independent applications

tions; take informal notes at conferences and store these in your planning journal.

Year Three: Develop and use Strategy Assessment Sheets; work with colleagues to develop a cross-grade plan for teaching strategies.

By slowly adding items to your record-keeping load, you will learn to manage the paper work and reserve time to reflect on your program.

Some Closing Thoughts

Readers benefit from frameworks, supportive strategies that enable them to solve reading problems and become proficient readers. It's the delight, the laughter, the tears, the sense that you have become a character that creates lifetime readers.

Jason, a fifth-grader, told me, "Reading is boring, I never understand the books we get. What's the point?" But at the end of sixth grade, Jason grinned when I read him that quote. "Well," he said, "now that reading is fun, I do it at home. Even got a library card, like you said I should a million times. My mom teases me and calls me a bookworm...but she's proud."

The strategic reading model provides students in all grades with opportunities to observe and practice strategies, apply them to a variety of reading materials, and, through debriefings, share what has been learned. Solving reading problems, absorbing and thinking with new information does not automatically occur from reading good books across the curriculum. Learners must first work together, then in small groups or with partners. The teacher is there, watching, prompting, encouraging, modeling, questioning, discussing, and spotlighting strategies and beneficial reading behaviors.

Growing lifetime readers takes time and practice and a commitment to developing a comprehensive reading program. The goal of a comprehensive reading program is to enable all children to read proficiently. Even more important, is to foster the desire to read beyond school assignments. Second-grader Emily Kinsey summed up these goals in her journal entry:

Rainy Days,

I like when it rains because I like to read. I unplug the T.V. and read and read and read !!!!!!

BIBLIOGRAPHY

Atwell, Nancie. *In the Middle: Writing, Reading and Learning with Adolescents.* Portsmouth, NH: Heinemann, 1987.

Barr, Rebecca, Marilyn Adow, and Camille Blachwicz. *Reading Diagnosis for Teachers: An Instructional Approach.* New York: Longman, 1990.

Calkins, Lucy. *The Art of Teaching Writing.* Portsmouth, NH: Heinemann, 1986.

Crafton, Linda K. *Whole Language: Getting Started...Moving Forward.* Katonah, New York: Richard C. Owen, 1991.

Gillet, Jean Wallace, and Charles Temple. *Understanding Reading Problems: Assessment and Instruction.* 3rd ed. Boston: Little Brown, 1991.

Heimlich, Joan E., and Susan D. Pittleman. *Semantic Mapping: Classroom Applications.* Newark, DE: International Reading Association, 1986.

Rosenblatt, Louise. *Literature as Exploration.* 4th ed. New York: The Modern Language Association of America, 1983.

Rosenblatt, Louise. *The Reader, the Text, the Poem: The Transactional Theory of the Literary Work.* Carbondale, IL: Southern Illinois University Press, 1978.

Robb, Laura. "A Cause for Celebration: Reading and Writing With At-Risk Children." *The New Advocate.* 6, no. 1 (Winter 1993): 25-40.

— *Whole Language, Whole Learners: Creating A Literature Centered Classroom.* New York: William Morrow, 1994.

Smith, Frank. *Reading Without Nonsense.* New York: Teachers College, Columbia University, 1978.

Vaughan Joseph L., and Thomas H. Estes. *Reading and Reasoning Beyond the Primary Grades.* Boston: Allyn and Bacon, 1986.

CHILDREN'S BOOKS CITED

Alexander, Lloyd. *The Book of Three.* New York: Bantam, Doubleday, Dell, 1964.

Baum, Frank. *The Wizard of Oz.* Woodstock, IL: Dramatic Publishing Company, 1963.

Begay, Shonto. "Our Mysteries, His Knowledge." From *Navaho: Visions and Voices Across the Mesa.* New York: Scholastic, 1995.

Byars, Betsy. *The Pinballs.* New York: Harper & Row, 1987.

Chiasson, John G. *African Journey.* New York: Bradbury, 1987.

Fleischman, Sid. *The Whipping Boy.* Illustrated by Peter Sis. New York: Greenwillow, 1986.

Hamilton, Virginia. *The Dark Way: Stories from the Spirit World.* New York: Harcourt, 1990.

Haskins, Jim. *Get On Board: The Story of the Underground Railroad.* New York: Scholastic, 1993

Kellogg, Steven. *Pecos Bill.* New York: William Morrow, 1986.

Leaf, Munro. *The Story of Ferdinand.* Drawings by Robert Lawson. New York: The Viking Press, 1938.

MacLachlan, Patricia. *Baby.* New York: Bantam, Doubleday, Dell, 1993.

— *Sarah, Plain and Tall.* New York: Harper & Row, 1985.

Osbourne, Mary Pope. *American Tall Tales.* Wood engravings by Michael

McCurdy. New York: Knopf, 1991.

Paterson, Katherine. *The Great Gilly Hopkins.* New York: Crowell, 1978.

Paterson, Katherine. *The Tale of the Mandarin Ducks.* Illustrated by Leo and Diane Dillon. New York: Lodestar, 1990.

Peterson, John. *The Littles.* New York: Scholastic, 1967.

Pilkey, Dav. *The Hallo-Wiener.* New York: Scholastic, 1995.

San Souci, Robert D. "Brother and Sister" and "The Ghostly Little Girl." From *Short & Shivery.* Illustrated by Katherine Coville. New York: Delcorte Press, 1987.

Schwartz, Alvin. *Stories To Tell A Cat.* Illustrated by Catherine Huerta. New York; HarperCollins, 1992.

Stevens, Carla. *Lily and Miss Liberty.* Illustrated by Deborah Kogan Ray. New York; Scholastic, 1992.

Taylor, Mildred D. *The Friendship.* Pictures by Max Grinsburg. New York: Dial Books For Young Readers, 1989.

NOTES

NOTES